GW00727922

SOLD
WITH OR WITHOUT
AN ESTATE AGENT

SOLD
WITH OR WITHOUT
AN ESTATE AGENT

by

Nicolas Savage

PAPERFRONTS
ELLIOT RIGHT WAY BOOKS
KINGSWOOD, SURREY, U.K.

Typeset in 10pt Times Roman by
EMS Photosetters, Rochford, Essex
Made and Printed in Great Britain by
Hartnolls Limited, Bodmin, Cornwall.

With thanks to Geraldine —
and Geoffrey "Burydell" Shreeves

Cartoons by Ebbarc

CONTENTS

WHO NEEDS AN ESTATE AGENT?

Estate agents are among the most unpopular people in the country. This book will not only point out some of their less lovable practices, but also help you understand why their business is not a particularly easy one to conduct.

If you want to use an agent to sell your property, it discusses the different types, how you should make your choice and the service you should expect for your money.

If you are looking for property, it tells you the best way to approach agents, builders and private sales. Special consideration must be given when trying to purchase property in need of renovation.

If you want to handle the sale of your own property, it tells you the methods most likely to succeed, and the problems that are likely to arise.

When I showed this book to the partner of a firm of estate agents he agreed that from his point of view it could only help to raise the general standard of estate agency, a prospect that did not alarm him as he provides a good service, but he did add that in telling people what is really involved in selling without an agent, I was going to put them off: people are under the impression it is so easy. I agree that it looks easy from the outside, but I think that this estate agent was underestimating people's intelligence, independence and desire to save money. Many people try to sell without an estate agent; careful study of this book will give them an enormously increased chance of success.

PROPERTY TERMS

APPLICANT

Person looking for property.

BRIDGING LOAN

A loan enabling a person to buy a property prior to selling his existing one.

BUILDING SOCIETY/ BANK SURVEY

Inspection and valuation carried out by a qualified surveyor on behalf of the lending house, to ensure the property represents sufficient security for the amount being borrowed.

CHAIN

Series of dependent property transactions.

CLIENT

Vendor employing an estate agent to act on his behalf. Vendor or purchaser employing solicitor or mortgage broker to act on his behalf.

COMPANY BRIDGING

A bridging loan as above, provided by a company in order to improve the mobility of its employees.

COMPLETION

Point at which the balance of the money is paid and the purchaser takes possession of the property.

CONTRACT RACE	When two or more contracts are sent out by the solicitor acting for the vendor of a property. First to exchange contracts gets the property.
CONVEYANCE	The legal process by which a property is transferred from one party to another.
EXCHANGE OF CONTRACTS	Point at which a commitment is made to a property transaction. A five or ten per cent deposit is paid by the purchaser and the completion date is fixed.
FULL STRUCTURAL SURVEY	Inspection and valuation carried out by a qualified surveyor on behalf of the proposed purchaser in order to give a detailed report on the structural condition. Can also include a schedule of work necessary to put it in good order if required.
GAZUMPING	Accepting a higher offer once a sale has been agreed in principle.
HOUSE/FLAT BUYERS REPORT	Inspection and valuation carried out by a qualified surveyor on behalf of a proposed purchaser. Cheaper and consequently less detailed than a full structural survey, this is sufficient for most properties that appear to be in good order, but will uncover anything unpleasant that might require further comment. Is often carried out at the same time as the building society/bank survey.

INSTRUCTION	Property being handled by an estate agent.
PROPOSED PURCHASER	An applicant who has indicated his willingness to purchase a property but has yet to commit himself.
SEARCHES	Enquiries made by a proposed purchaser's solicitor to the local authority relating to any planning proposals, new roads, etc., that might affect his client's proposed purchase.
STAMP DUTY	Tax paid by the purchaser of a property. It does not apply to properties being bought at prices up to £30,000. Over £30,000 the purchaser pays 1% of the total purchase price.
VENDOR	Person selling property.

1

THE NATURE OF
ESTATE AGENCY

The system that has evolved over the years is extremely inefficient. It is rendered more so by the prolonged and unnecessarily cumbersome conveyancing process that runs alongside. Property owners in Scotland are fortunate in that at least they do not have the anxiety, uncertainty and potential inefficiencies of the contract stage that exist in England and Wales, since offers are not made subject to contract – they are legally binding.

Unfortunately it is not possible to say what level of fees estate agents would charge if a more efficient system was introduced, but suffice to say, they would bear no relation to those existing today. In order to understand why fees are so high, it is necessary to understand the problems an agent has to overcome.

The property market has always tended to be seasonal with the result that staffing levels are a problem. During the busy periods there is never enough time to do everything but a reasonable number of people have to be employed to keep standards high. During the quiet periods, holidays, Christmas, etc., the highly paid managers, negotiators, secretaries and receptionists have little to do but they still draw their pay cheques. Commission-related earnings go some way to relieve this, but the effect is minor. Advertising, although reduced, has to be continued during the quiet periods in order to maintain a presence in the public eye and the constant outgoings, rent, rates, insurance, etc., are a continual drain. The successful sales in the busy periods have to finance the times of loss.

Even during the periods of great activity the estate agent is forced to waste large amounts of money. He does a lot of work on properties that do not sell and has to put up with large numbers of time-wasters. There are vendors and proposed purchasers who for genuine business or personal reasons are forced to change their plans; to these must be added vendors who enjoy having their property on the market as a sort of confirmation of status; vendors who just test the market by putting their property up at a ridiculously high price; vendors with an inflated idea of their purchasing power who change their minds when they cannot buy the property they expected; vendors whose move depends on an unlikely chain of events but want a buyer on the off-chance and so on; vendors with nothing to lose by their actions. An estate agent will rarely turn down an instruction to sell a property . . . just in case. There are the time-wasting applicants too – those who stay on mailing lists constantly just to see what is about and those who view properties out of nosiness: some make low offers for several properties in the hope that one vendor might be desperate, some continue to view property when they have agreed a purchase already and others are frightened off a property by ludicrously trivial points raised in a survey. Some applicants become well-known by local agents as time-wasters but they stay on their lists . . . just in case.

To put the problem into numerical perspective, out of every 100 properties an agent is invited to value, he might be instructed to sell 40. Out of that 40, after advertising, circulation of details, showing applicants round etc., 20 might find prospective purchasers, 5 of whom may fall by the wayside prior to exchange of contracts. Out of every 100 sets of details circulated, 10 may result in enquiries and 4 in appointments. The categories for applicants' requirements are wide, so an attitude of blanket coverage prevails . . . just in case.

If you then bear in mind the duplication of advertising, details' circulation and staff activity caused by properties on the market with more than one agent, it makes one wonder how agents manage to keep their fees so low. It is the successful sales that pay for the whole affair and ensure it is worthwhile for the agent to perform his expensive and often futile gyrations. Contrary to popular belief, estate agents work long and hard for their money. It is highly lucrative for some, but the undeniable fact is that estate agency is disproportionately expensive to the service it provides the vendors whose properties do actually sell.

It must be stressed that the majority of estate agents are averagely honest businessmen, not the pompous professionals or shifty wide boys as they are so often labelled, but they are all subject to temptations that are not entirely in their client's interest and some succumb. One should be aware of the points at which these temptations arise – these are outlined in the following chapters.

2

BEFORE YOU SELL

Many factors have to be considered prior to making the decision to move your home, following which you will want to give yourself the best chance possible of selling at the highest price, whether you decide to use an estate agent or not. Included in this chapter is the basis of contract procedure as this is a good time to refresh your memory.

How Much Does it Cost to Move?
It is vital to work out your costs as accurately as possible before deciding to move. This involves obtaining estimates in most instances.

Estate Agents
Fees are payable by the vendor upon completion of the transaction. A few telephone calls will give you an idea of fee levels in your area – remember that V.A.T. will be payable. If you are not using an agent, make a suitable allowance for advertising – always estimate on the pessimistic side and you can only be pleased when you spend less.

Solicitors
Ask for a fixed price – make sure it includes building society legal fees and Land Registry fees. He is likely to

want to know the approximate prices you are proposing to buy and sell at. V.A.T. is payable again.

Valuers

Details of building society or bank scale valuation fees can be obtained from the organisation in question. Remember that most banks charge an arrangement fee. V.A.T. is usually inclusive, but check.

Surveyors

The cost of a House Buyers Report is dictated by a fixed scale based on the value of the property. A local surveyor will be happy to give you the necessary information. A Full Structural Survey is considerably more expensive, but if you have any doubts about the condition of the property and would prefer a more detailed survey, describe the type of thing you have in mind to a surveyor and he will give you a range of expected cost. You can, of course, commission any level of survey between a House Buyers Report and a Full Structural Survey, e.g. if you suspect a fault in a particular area and you want that alone checked out in detail. V.A.T. is payable.

Stamp Duty

If your purchase is likely to be under £30,000 you will be exempt. If it is likely to be over, Stamp Duty is payable on the full purchase price at the rate of 1%.

Removals

Obtain three quotes. They may need to be updated by the time you move, but the difference is unlikely to be significant. V.A.T. is payable.

Is it Worthwhile Moving?

If the costs are within your expectations, the next question to ask yourself is your motive for moving. Establish your approximate borrowing capacity by having a word with your building society or bank and ensure you are going to feel comfortable with the increased repayments. Look at the properties that are within your new price range – do they fit in with your motives? It might make more sense to extend your existing property within your capability. Moving your home is a difficult and expensive affair at the best of times so make sure you are doing it for the right reasons. The cost of carpets and curtains must also be considered, as well as furniture which may be needed; these things add up to very large amounts.

Timing

The best time to buy and sell is when the greatest number of people are trying to buy and sell. In the past, Spring has been the busiest period, possibly to tie in with a move at the end of the school year, perhaps because it was felt that applicants would be reluctant to view properties in the gloomy months of January and February and vendors wanted to show their properties when their gardens looked less like something from the Battle of the Somme. If your outlook or garden is spectacularly improved by the addition of leaves to the trees then it can be worth waiting, otherwise market your property as close to the New Year as you like, since this is when the real activity begins. This change in attitude is thought to be caused by the impression that prices always rise in the Spring, with the result that applicants have been coming to the market earlier and earlier to beat the increase and scaling up market activity as a consequence. There is also the theory that people like to move in Spring or early Summer to give themselves time to settle in and carry out any alterations before the following Winter. Whatever the reasons, there is no argument against marketing your property in the first six months of the year.

If you leave it until late June to start, you are going to be cutting it a bit fine as the Summer holiday period is unarguably going to affect the numbers of people active within the market. From the second week in July to the second week in September large chunks of the population are so busy looking after children, they haven't the time, or are just about to go on holiday, are on holiday or have just returned and are recovering. It is a process which peaks in August when in many areas it would be cheaper for agents to shut their offices.

Going on from there, September, October and November are all active months as a rule, but less reliably so, owing to people's reluctance to move over the Christmas period. December falls into the same category as August when only the few people who are having to move for one reason or another will be active – once again the market shrinks and estate agents spend long periods twiddling their thumbs or attending office parties.

It is worth highlighting at this point the difficult position an agent is put in when asked the best time a property should be marketed. He knows perfectly well when the good and bad periods are, but it takes an agent who is very confident of his client's allegiance to advise say, on July 7th that a property should be withheld from the market until September 14th. Many will not as they can imagine only too clearly the persuasive enthusiasm a rival would muster in advising that the property should be marketed at once with his agency – an instruction over a quiet period is better than no instruction.

Do not take the attitude that it is not going to do any harm to put your property on the market over the quiet periods – you will lose all the initial impact of your advertising and a property which has been on the market for weeks tempts the opinion that 'there must be something wrong with it', whether this is deserved or not. Additionally, if you are using an agent, his enthusiasm for a property wanes as he sees it on his register week after week (it is not unusual for such properties to be referred to as 'Turkeys').

As a final point, if there is an uncertain factor relating to planning hanging over your property like the Sword of Damocles (e.g. a new motorway twenty metres away) wait until it is resolved one way or the other if at all possible. If you do not, it is likely that the price you expect to achieve will be based on the assumption that it is not going to be built and the price applicants will expect to pay will assume that it is going ahead and ne'er the twain shall meet.

Sell First or Buy First?

This depends on the market in your area, your circumstances and the type of property you are trying to buy and sell. Remember always that you want to put yourself in the strongest possible bargaining position and in the majority of cases this means finding a buyer first. Estate agents tend to meet resistance when they make this suggestion as vendors worry about being pressurised by potential purchasers. Do not worry; you are selling so you determine the pace.

Whether property moves quickly in your area or not, if you are looking for a straightforward property, sell first. In the case of a fast-moving area the chances are that two or three people are going to be interested in the property you want to buy and you must be in as strong a position as possible to give yourself the best chance of having your offer accepted. In the slow-moving area it is unlikely that your offer will be taken seriously or that the vendor will take his property off the market unless you have a proposed purchaser.

In both instances, however, an exception must be made when you are looking for something out of the ordinary, as it is possible that in lining up a prospective purchaser long before you start to proceed on your own purchase, you run the risk of underselling because the market has moved on. Of course, sometimes it takes a long time to find a property even in a busy market – perhaps as a result of unlucky choices of property where the vendors are unable to proceed. Do not expect your estate agent to come to you and tell you that your property is now undervalued; it will be up to you to keep an eye on prices for similar properties and if the gap becomes noticeable, let the agent know what you want to do about it. If he argues, get the property valued by another reliable agent. In the event of an unacceptable discrepancy, ask your agent to explain the situation in a tactful manner to your proposed purchaser who should be given first chance to buy at the new price. If he says no, instruct the agent to remarket.

Should you be moving from a fast-moving area like the Home Counties or London to an area in the North where property sells at a more sedate pace, you can afford to find your property first – most agents, wherever they are in business, are aware of the speed of sales in the Home Counties and London and will be happy to reassure their clients on this point.

Look at the frequency with which properties of the type you intend to buy and sell come on the market. If you are looking for a three bedroom cottage of a type that is in relative abundance and are selling a five bedroom house in an area where such properties are like hen's teeth, you can afford the luxury of choosing your property at leisure and then asking prospective purchasers to form an orderly queue. It is essential to make sure that your agent will enthusiastically vouch for the instant saleability of your house.

The points to remember are that selling first should allow you to proceed at once, reducing the risk of gazumping, putting you in a better negotiating position and giving you a firm idea of what you can spend. Nobody can pressurise you into moving faster than you want to.

If you are in the fortunate position of not needing to co-ordinate your sale and purchase because you have company or other bridging finance, then obviously you can look at your own pace, safe in the knowledge that you are in an excellent bargaining position, and then market your own property when you are ready. If you wish to maximise the financial gain to be made from such a facility, make sure that you find a situation where being in such a position is of greatest value to the vendor. A note of caution on the sale – do not delay matters too long as most properties sell best whilst still lived in; they tend to look a bit frayed at the edges once the furniture has been taken out, even if they were decorated the previous year. Do your sums too, so that you know how much per week a bridging loan is likely to cost you personally, for which you can make a realistic budgeting allowance.

Bearing in mind the negotiating strength to be gained from breaking the chain, it is worth putting up with the inconvenience of staying with parents or friends if at all possible. Chains are one of the blights on property transactions in England and Wales, so break yours if you can. Should you be able to do so, you will be just another buyer in a good position at first, but as your sale progresses you will become more and more attractive to a vendor who is keen to sell and, once you have exchanged contracts, you are in as strong a position as the buyer with company bridging. Once more, beware of leaving too long a gap between the two transactions as you may lose your financial advantage if prices move onward and upward.

As a final point, it is advisable to instruct your solicitor to move slowly on either sale or purchase until such time as you have tied up the other side of the transaction. Anything can happen and there is no point in incurring any significant expenses before it is absolutely necessary.

Presentation of Your Property
Whatever you are selling, be it a car, a piano or a refrigerator, presentation is important. Property is no exception. You would not try to sell your car when it was dirty or cluttered up so don't try and do it with your property. A thorough Spring-clean is a minimum requirement. Do all those small repairs you have been putting off. Wash the windows to let in more light. If your property has become cluttered up because you have outgrown it, then create the impression of more space and store some excess furniture in the garage, loft, or with friends – leave as little as possible to the applicant's imagination. If you have open fires and the season is right, light them. Make your property as appealing as possible. In the garden, smarten everything up, mend the fence, cut back any shrubs that have become overgrown, especially if they are blocking the light into the house – make sure it looks its size.

Decoration is another problem. Ideally, your property should be newly decorated in neutral shades (unless you have a very good eye for co-ordination) but, understandably, few people are prepared to go to that trouble or expense at this juncture. If your property is in good condition with the exception of one room it is worth bringing it up to standard to round off the general impression, but if you have let the whole property get rather shabby, there is no point in decorating one or two rooms as you are just going to show up the rest – unless you are going to paint everywhere, a thorough clean will be enough. Similarly with exterior decoration – if it gives a shabby impression and the interior is in good order, bring it up to standard.

Any further work is of debatable value. Only very rarely does an extension repay its cost at once. Circumstances when this is likely are when a property is out of balance, e.g. having three reception rooms and only two bedrooms – a family house downstairs and a single's or couple's house upstairs. Gas central heating repays itself in most cases but remember that you will probably have to redecorate as a result. Double glazing and cavity wall insulation will only occasionally repay their costs at once, so do not have either of these jobs carried out just to enhance your sale. As a general rule carry out any major improvement for yourself – make sure you have the benefit before passing it onto somebody else.

As an example of this, consider a common problem for estate agents which arises when they encounter a vendor who has seen virtually the same property as his sell for £50,000 and expects his property to be worth £65,000 or more because he has recently spent £15,000 on an extension. The chances are that it is worth less than £60,000.

Solicitor, Conveyancing Company or D.I.Y.?
If you are considering doing your own conveyancing, read up on the subject very carefully before you make your decision. You will have to be very thorough and are taking on an important task. There will be no comeback if you get it wrong. Only too frequently when a vendor deals with his own conveyancing he ends up delaying matters and needs assistance from one of the solicitors involved.

Conveyancing companies are usually a bit cheaper than solicitors and, in the same way as going it alone, work well as long as nothing out of the ordinary happens.

Remember that your building society will still want to instruct a solicitor to deal with their interests in the transaction.

Whilst writing this book, licensed conveyancers were just about to come onto the scene. The word is that the building societies will be prepared to instruct them to deal with their interests. If they appear in your area, ask your local agents if they are any good; they may well be

Solicitors are still the most reliable way of transferring property from one person to another. Naturally there are good and bad, so ask around for recommendations and get estimates. It is important to find somebody you have confidence in and you must communicate well with each other, so avoid the man you find intimidating. A local solicitor is an advantage for his knowledge of the area and the likelihood is that he is going to be more realistic about fees. It is desirable to find a solicitor that will not make any charge if the sale does not go through.

Once you have decided which course you intend to take, it is a good idea to apply (or in the case of a solicitor or conveyancing company get them to apply) for the deeds of your property from the bank or building society that is keeping them. Check how long Local Authority Searches take in your area too; if it is more than four weeks (and in some areas it is considerably longer) apply for them – the fee is less than £20 and will be passed onto the purchaser. Both of these precautions might save you valuable time during the contract stage. A Search is valid for 90 days from the date of issue, so if you live in an area where you cannot reasonably expect to sell within that period, hold back on this course.

Contract Procedure
When you purchased your present property your worry and confusion may have been multiplied by not

understanding the process – even if you did, the chances are it was some time ago so it will do you no harm to refresh your memory.

Once solicitors are put in touch, four principal procedures are set into action simultaneously. The proposed purchaser's solicitor will apply to the Local Authority for Searches (unless you already have them in hand) and will request a draft contract from the vendor's solicitor. The proposed purchaser will make his mortgage application and organise a House or Flat Buyers Report or Full Structural Survey.

Searches

The responses to the Searches will be returned to the proposed purchaser's solicitor in due course (the period depends on the Local Authority) and he will advise his client of any problems that might have arisen. If there is a major planning proposal in the vicinity, the proposed purchaser will be advised to examine the plans which will be available for this purpose at the Local Authority offices and consequently decide if he still wishes to proceed. In most cases Searches reveal no problems.

Contract

Once the proposed purchaser's solicitor has received the draft contract, he makes the Enquiries Before Contract which consist of a standard list of questions relating to boundaries, disputes, guarantees, services, planning permission and so forth. The vendor's solicitor will answer these to the best of his ability in conjunction with the vendor and forward the responses back to the proposed purchaser's solicitor. Inevitably questions will arise from the answers given, but once these have been cleared up the contract is said to be approved. Make sure you know what additional features, such as carpets are included in the sale, and that this information is detailed in the contract.

The title, i.e. rightful ownership of the property, has to be established by the purchaser's solicitor for his client and the lending house involved. If it is properly registered at the Land Registry this presents no problem – if not, it will have to be traced back for at least fifteen years before the solicitor is happy. In both cases, the purchaser's solicitor will be verifying that the title refers to the same property that his client thinks he is buying.

The assignment of leasehold property is rather more complex, since the lease will contain many maintenance regulations, restrictive covenants (e.g. no pets) and relates to other parties – the freeholder and other leaseholders. Copies of the three previous years Management Accounts have to be obtained from the management company or managing agents, and approved. In some cases the proposed leaseholder has to get permission from the freeholder to take over the lease. This is rarely withheld. Title has to be established in the same way as with freehold property.

Mortgage

It is likely that the proposed purchaser's building society or bank will be willing to instruct his solicitor to act for them at the same time as dealing with the conveyancing matters. This is to be encouraged as it saves duplication of work and hence time.

When the mortgage application form is sent to the building society/bank with the appropriate survey fee, a surveyor will be appointed and make his inspection whilst the references given on the form are being verified. The surveyor will give his opinion of value which will lean towards the cautious side and is principally to ensure the security of the loan, so make sure that you have your own valuation too. In the case of a property with problems such as damp, woodworm, faulty roof or wiring, he will recommend that a retention of funds be made until the faults are rectified. This is not unusual and a short-term bank loan can usually be taken while the work is carried out. Subject to availability of funds, satisfactory return of references and there being no problems on survey, the proposed purchaser will be sent a written offer of mortgage, a copy of which should be sent to his solicitor. The proposed purchaser's solicitor will not advise exchange of contracts unless he is certain his client has sufficient funds to complete the transaction.

House and Flat Buyers Report and Full Structural Survey
A House Buyers Report can be carried out by the surveyor carrying out the building society valuation and time is saved by instructing him to do so. A Full Structural Survey is a lengthier affair in every sense, but again it could be done by the same person. In both instances the proposed purchaser should lose no time in having them carried out. If he is the sort that is easily scared by trivial points raised in a survey, all parties involved want to know quickly so that as little time and money is wasted as possible. Similarly if the survey raises genuine grievances, one requires plenty of time to resolve them.

It is likely that the proposed purchaser's solicitor will ask him to make a personal appearance to ensure that he understands the contract he is about to sign and anything that might have been raised by the Searches and Enquiries Before Contract. Once he is happy in this respect he will require instructions regarding completion (the day agreed between his client and the vendor for possession). The contract can now be signed.

A deposit will be requested by the vendor's solicitor.

This is likely to be five or ten per cent of the purchase price, depending on the solicitors involved. In the case of a purchaser obtaining a 100% mortgage, the deposit is obtained from the building society or bank. If a vendor wishes to use his purchaser's deposit as part of the deposit on his own purchase, as often happens, permission has to be given by the purchaser's solicitor.

Once the proposed purchaser's solicitor has the signed contract and deposit, he will forward them to the vendor's solicitor with instructions for them to be held to order, effectively awaiting a telephone call to formalise exchange of contracts. This call will be made when every party to the transaction is ready to go.

When contracts have been exchanged, the parties are committed to the transaction and all that remains for them to be concerned about is their imminent move. Do understand that the commitment is total. You would certainly lose your deposit were you to withdraw; if you completed late you would be charged interest on the completion monies at a penal rate (this is noted in the contract). A vendor has a considerable armoury of steps he can take against a purchaser who cannot complete his commitment. Your solicitor can advise you of the potential outcome should you ever get into difficulties on this score. The solicitors still have work to do in the form of drawing up a Conveyance (if the land is unregistered), a Transfer (if the land is registered), or an Assignment (if the property is leasehold) and getting the relevant document signed, plus ensuring that the mortgage finance is to hand ready for the completion day.

On completion day, the remaining ninety or ninety-five per cent of the purchase price will be transferred to the vendor's solicitor. Once he is in receipt of this, he will authorise the release of the keys and the purchaser can take possession.

3

CHOOSING AN ESTATE AGENT

Professional or Non-Professional?
Before looking at the estate agencies of different sizes, which can be loosely divided into Small Practices (1 to 5 offices), Medium Practices (6 to 25 offices) and Large Practices (25+ offices), it is interesting to look at the difference between Professional and Non-Professional Firms.

An estate agency is justified in calling itself Professional if most of the partners are qualified, i.e. Fellows or Associates of the Royal Institute of Chartered Surveyors (F.R.I.C.S. or A.R.I.C.S.), or Fellows or Associates of the Society of Valuers and Auctioneers (F.S.V.A. or A.S.V.A.). To obtain these qualifications examinations must now be passed but some of the older members will have been admitted when an organisation that did not require such high standards was absorbed by the organisation involved. These people are often the most vociferous critics of Non-Professional Firms. The examinations are strict and demonstrate a high degree of knowledge in many areas of property: knowledge which enables the person to execute the tasks which, quite correctly, should only be carried out by a person qualified to do so (examples in the residential area being House Buyers Reports and Full Structural Surveys) and with proper indemnity insurance which these people will have.

However the qualification covers many aspects of property work, industrial, commercial, town planning to name but a few, which is all very well but is that much use to the residential estate agent? The fact is that relatively few qualified people are involved in the active marketing of residential property. In the case of the Professional Firm, the partner in charge of residential agency will be qualified but the chances are that he will busy himself more with residential development land and surveys and valuations than anything else, and the residential agency work will be dealt with by unqualified people.

Both the R.I.C.S. and I.S.V.A. do have strict codes of practice which have to be observed by everybody within a firm of which the qualified person is a member. So does the National Association of Estate Agents (N.A.E.A.) which has many Non-Professional Firms as members. The qualifications for becoming a Fellow or Associate of the N.A.E.A. are 7 or 3 years' experience respectively with a reputable firm and an interview with a Board during which some fairly basic questions are asked. The code of practice in all three organisations is a safeguard that you are not dealing with a known crook but inevitably in all cases there are people who sail close to the wind so it is not an excuse for complacency in their clients. A firm should not be dismissed if it is not a member of any of these organisations – just look at it a little more carefully.

A Non-Professional Firm can be set up by anybody, but they are usually started by experienced people with confidence in their abilities to succeed. It is an expensive exercise starting a new agency from scratch and a person would be foolhardy to attempt it without at least three years in the business.

To sum up. An estate agent does not need to be qualified to be good at selling residential property – he needs experience (helped by training within the firm if possible) and he needs flair (which nobody can teach him). A recently qualified person can be a dead loss, only seeing it as a necessary drudge before going on to an activity that makes better use of his qualifications. A young person who left school with no qualifications can have the enthusiasm and natural flair which makes him a credit to any office

If you are selling an unusual property, it is worth looking for a specialist agent as well as using a local. This applies in particular to expensive country houses where it is advisable to consult the London agents with specific departments and a wide overall knowledge of the market. Be warned though, their services do not come cheap.

In Professional and Non-Professional Firms each office is only as good as the people working in it.

Small Practices (1 to 5 offices)
These can vary from the crusty old chap sitting in his dingy office to the keen young man in his mid-twenties who has risked so much to set up his bright new venture. There are many types in between and one could not hope to categorise all of them but hopefully this will help to put many into perspective. In all cases, unless the agency is a total dud, you should get an acceptable service if you know an employee or partner personally.

The elderly gentleman has probably had thirty years' experience in the area and will have sold many of the properties in it three or four times over. He is quite likely to be offhand with applicants after half a lifetime of time-wasters. It is quite possible that he has been very involved locally and will know an awful lot of people in the area. Such practices tend to deal with a small turnover of the high quality properties in an area, providing the owner with a comfortable, but not spectacular, living. He will not appear to be worried whether he gets instructed to

I KNOW IT'S A GOOD HOUSE
I'VE SOLD IT ELEVEN TIMES
IN 40 YEARS.

"CRUSTY OLD AGENT OF 50 YEARS
IN THE LOCALITY."

sell your property or not. In fact you may end up feeling
that he is doing you a favour by accepting your property
on his register. His extensive knowledge of the area and its
inhabitants are his main assets. On the other hand, his
advertising budget is likely to be small and details poor.
Do not expect enthusiasm after so long in the business
and watch his valuations as they will tend to be low.
Although he is likely to be on Christian name terms with
many of the local solicitors, do not expect too much
attention during the contract stage.

A similar type but a few years younger may have a
rather more up-to-date attitude to advertising. details
etc., which will be helped by the employment of a
manager to take care of the day-to-day running of the
residential agency This gentleman is likely to be involved

locally in Rotary, Chamber of Commerce, Freemasons etc. He may even be a Magistrate. The chances are that this pillar of society is more concerned with local development (especially if it is his own land) and commercial property, having eased himself gently out of the residential side. The manager is unlikely to have fire in his heart, as this would offend his employer but will probably run the office in an efficient and stable manner. The good name of the firm is paramount to these people and they will be openly contemptuous of the newer agencies and their methods. Once again the local knowledge is going to help the firm, and the manager is likely to have a better idea of values than his employer, but the reality is that the manager, although quite confident, lacks the enthusiasm to impress, relying too much on the good name and possibly the qualifications of his employer. If you are concerned about potential trickery by your agency, the pillar of society and his minion are for you, but be prepared for a less than perfect service during the contract stage as they will take the old-fashioned attitude that these things are best left to solicitors.

Occasionally you might encounter a similar type who is relatively recently established, having been retired from a larger agency or another business. He is not out to make a fortune and is very likely to 'play with a straight bat'. Take a look at this fellow – he has learnt the business more recently, is obviously quite bright and will still have some enthusiasm for the job. As a result he could be very good at it.

Going on from there we consider the established modern agencies. These tend to be quite clued up on marketing methods but their efficiency and enthusiasm will depend to a large extent on the ability, commitment and ambition of the principal or partners. Look closely at the agency where the day-to-day running is left in the hands of employees and the principal appears to be semi-retired or interested in other businesses. It may be at the stage where the principal has made a very good living for some years, is no longer 'hungry' and is bored, letting matters drift. The nature of the business allows an agency to survive on reputation for a long time. When looking at small agencies it is important to look for a partner or principal keeping a very close eye on his employees as there is no substitute for the drive of somebody who has an interest in the business. The expanding small agency is well worth looking at; it is expanding for a reason, which is that it is making enough money to set up new offices and its principal or partners are ambitious. They know

.... MAKE SURE THAT SOMEBODY IS KEEPING A CLOSE EYE ....

how to run an agency in order to make money and that means selling property. The worst of these is the unscrupulous type who cares nothing for his reputation, or that of his profession, encouraging gazumping and so on. These agencies deal principally with the lower end of the market except in London where they can be found in any fast-moving area. They do not give a jot for their client's interests and are a menace.

The best of the expanding small agencies may well be the most efficient in the area. They are making money because they are advising their clients properly, presenting the properties well, negotiating deals and holding them together by keeping a close eye on them during the contract stage. The principal or a partner will be breathing down everybody's neck to ensure they are doing their job properly. With any of the modern agencies you will lack the thorough knowledge of the area that the pillar of society will have, but what they do not know the good ones will find out, just by asking about.

The very new agencies are a bit of an unknown quantity. You can be assured of their enthusiasm certainly, and the chances are that they will have a good advertising presence to make their name known. On the other hand, their reputations will have yet to become clear and if they are totally new to the area, their valuations may not be reliable. If they have moved from an existing agency in the area, take a look at their former employers as you can usually count on some of their attitudes and practices rubbing off.

The only other variation worth mentioning is the small professional and commercial agency. Residential agency is likely to be more of a sideline to these people – they might even seem surprised that you are contemplating instructing them. If you think your property might have some development potential bring them in, otherwise forget it.

Medium Practices (6 to 25 offices)

These consist for the most part of what were the more
successful expanding small agencies a few years ago.
Because of their greater size they tend to be less extreme in
their attitudes i.e. less unscrupulous or less meticulous –
the partners can no longer keep such a keen eye on what
goes on and have appointed managers. The managers
bear the brunt of any scrutiny from the partners and are
expected to transmit the attitudes of their peers to the
negotiators but inevitably the managers' interpretations
and commitment will colour these. Running twenty
offices on this basis is bound to dilute the ability of the
partners, however good they are, so it is important to look
for the firms that have taken in new partners to make sure
that somebody with a stake is still keeping a close eye on
things. The ideal is an active partner in each office.

Estate agencies of this size have bulk purchase facilities
and a strong negotiating position when it comes to
advertising which will save money that is likely to be spent
on promoting their corporate image to impress potential
clients. Some produce their own property paper which
again is quite impressive and quite a relevant aid to sales
where circulated widely in an indifferent market. When
the market is moving quickly, however, most of the
properties are likely to be under offer by the time the
paper is delivered (usually monthly). The value of these
papers is considerable in areas without a focal point for
local adveritisng.

A principal advantage of medium practices should lie
in the interaction between offices, passing on relevant
applicants, information and instructions, but many fail to
take full advantage of this because of inter-office rivalry.
Without a doubt this is a problem where the offices are
just run by managers – they are going to be vying with
each other for the best monthly figures and personal

animosities often arise between colleagues. Imagine a situation where office A is instructed to sell a property. It will be offered in office A of course and eventually, in office B in the adjacent town. If offers for the property are received in both offices, the manager or negotiator in office A, who will be submitting the offers will have a greater financial incentive to get his own offer accepted than he will that of office B. Office A is thereby tempted to exaggerate the merits of his own offer, because of this conflict of interests – the client's interests are at stake as a result. Sometimes this competition can be as strong, and therefore as detrimental to the client, as that between two separate firms. This is an extremely difficult problem for a firm to overcome without abolishing incentives totally, but it is likely to be less trouble if there is a partner in each office who will be wary of harming the firm's reputation as a whole.

Some firms have started to franchise their offices, which gives individuals the opportunity to own their own office outright with the advantage of retaining the protective umbrella of an impressive corporate image. They have to be carefully chosen to conduct themselves in the proper manner and maintain the standards of the whole, as one bad apple can taint the whole basket. Franchising does nothing to add to the incentive to co-operate with other offices though, and their actual advantage over a small practice must be carefully examined.

It is likely that medium practices will take advantage of possible peripheral business opportunities by setting up surveying departments, mortgage departments, insurance departments, removal firms, possibly even conveyancing – for the most part these are to the clients' advantage.

Large Practices (25+ offices)
Here we encounter a relatively new phenomenon – many small and medium practices have been purchased by public companies, mostly in the financial services sector, and built up into huge chains, linked by one corporate image. These organisations see estate agency not only as a potentially profitable business in itself, but also as an outlet for their mortgage and insurance departments.

These are early days to make too much comment on their effect on estate agency as a whole, and it would appear that the same potential advantages and conflicts apply to the general linking of offices as with the medium practice – it is a difficult problem to overcome.

The large practices have considerable advertising budgets at their disposal, giving them access to media that could not be considered by smaller firms, the most powerful of which is television. Advertising on this scale is primarily for the purpose of bringing in instructions and is of little value to you if the firm is selling your property. Similarly, their ability to point to several hundred offices around the country is of little use, since most people move locally – it does impress some potential vendors though.

It is worth remembering that these public companies have a reputation to protect from the word go. Bearing in mind that estate agency does not have a particularly good reputation, this can only mean that the corporate name under which all these small fry have been gathered will be kept as clean as possible. The directors will be at pains to protect and enhance their company's image at the point it comes into contact with the public – by training the staff. They will ensure a standard of competence within any office that cannot be guaranteed elsewhere. In smaller practices new employees have to be trained by partners and managers on the job, with all the potential disasters and embarrassments that may ensue, often at their client's expense. Under such circumstances the pupil is also likely to pick up the bad habits of those training him. Refresher courses for existing staff and comprehensive training for juniors can at least make the client feel assured that the person negotiating on his behalf has been told the best way to conduct himself. Training schemes do not necessarily make good estate agents, only experience can do that, but it should weed out the bad ones. Do remember that not all the large firms do train staff, so watch for it or you may find yourself in the position of the vendor who had his house valued by a young fellow who had been thrown in at the deep end – after one week's experience.

The large practices will certainly have a separate mortgage advisory service which can be useful. Whether it is going to be 100% independent of the estate agency department all the time is debatable, but it will certainly not be less so than the smaller agent, who refers his mortgage enquiries to a friendly broker who gives him a commission on any resulting insurance policies.

One company has even used its financial muscle in an attempt to tackle the blight that chains put on the property market. Although the sentiment is admirable, in practice it is unlikely to make any significant impact since the vendor using the service will only receive 90% of the valuation figure of his property.

These large practices are well worth looking at as they can be very good, but look at your local office on its own merit and particularly that of its staff and resist the temptation to be impressed by the size of the firm.

Computer-Linked Multi-Listing
The majority of medium and large practices are internally computer-linked to various extents, giving them added speed and ease of transfer of information but there is an

additional aspect to this facility which has arisen over the past few years that is well worth watching. It can loosely be described as multi-listing, although it does not take the comprehensive form as in the U.S.A.

Worried by the advent of the huge, City-backed practices, some small and medium practices have been joining up under a single corporate identity, whilst retaining their individual ownership and identities, and linking their offices by computer. They give access to their properties to other members, increasing the number of outlets enormously. The commission split is usually 60% to the firm that is instructed and 40% to the firm that introduces the buyer. In addition to the combined advertising strength this gives the firms involved, it can mean that your property will be offered at three or four offices within the relevant area giving multiple agency coverage at a sole agency price.

Whilst the aforementioned form of computer-linked multi-listing was instituted as a defensive measure against the newly formed conglomerates, another has arisen in London, backed by agents who are already highly successful and only seek to improve their service to the public. It was originally based on the co-operation that exists between some agents but has made this more widespread and efficient. The agents can claim that in addition to their usual personal service, and at sole agency rates, their properties can be offered in hundreds of other agents' offices around London. Add to this supportive advertising by the multi-listing firm to increase public awareness and there is a very powerful incentive to vendors to instruct agents with the facility.

Although still in its infancy, this is a very interesting development and a genuine aid to agents, vendors and applicants. Potentially it is the future of estate agency.

Miscellaneous

Estate agency has long been viewed from the outside as a gravy-train and all and sundry try to climb aboard from time to time. Department stores are likely to be restricted by the hours the whole store closes – agencies as a rule close late. Some solicitors may think that it is worth the trouble and stay with it but they are likely to be few in numbers. The services that require payment up front such as property shops and computer-matching are more of an aid to the vendor who is selling himself and probably take more business from the newspapers than anywhere else.

Businessmen of varying ability have been trying to change the system over the years – so far nobody has, but they will keep on trying.

Short-Listing Your Agents

When considering the sale of your property through an estate agent the first stage is usually to invite three or four agents to inspect and give their opinion of value. Choosing the three or four is your first problem – eliminate agents that do not advertise properly – eliminate agents that do not appear to deal with your type of property. Out of those left it is advisable to look at an agent from each category plus another that appeals from personal recommendation, good image, etc. Do not make the mistake of thinking an agent is the best because he has a lot of boards out – all that means is that at that time he has been given permission to put up boards by a large number of the clients on his books. Position of the agent's office is relevant, more from the point of view of speed than anything else. Most proposed purchasers come from advertising but inevitably the office located next to Marks and Spencer is going to pick up a larger percentage of the remainder than one tucked away in an alley (it cannot be denied that the agent in the better position sells more

properties, but this is principally because vendors are impressed by the position and as a result they tend to get more instructions). Most agencies tend to cluster in secondary positions among the opticians, travel agencies and employment agencies.

Having made your shortlist, take a look at them 'incognito'. Look at their offices – a smart office may not help to sell your house much but it does reflect an attitude

"TAKE A LOOK AT THEM INCOGNITO"

to the business. The atmosphere of an office is important, lethargy, cynicism and enthusiasm are all highly contagious. Look at the standard of their details – if you really want to be sure, speak to clients of the agencies and ask if they are satisfied with the service they are getting. Unfortunately it is unlikely that an agent will encourage you to speak to his clients and even if he does allow it, he is hardly likely to suggest you speak to someone that he is not on good terms with, so if you really want to pursue this course you will have to call uninvited at properties and be very polite as you explain your reasons. Details sheets and For Sale boards will be useful but more importantly, speak to someone who has Under Offer or Sold Provisionally on the board outside his property; he will have had plenty of opportunity to see the agent in action. Finally it does no harm to test the inter-office co-ordination if this is important to you, so contact the large, medium or computer-linked firm and ask for details of a property in an adjacent town.

These enquiries and tests will give you an idea of what to expect when you invite the agents to value your property.

Valuation and Making Your Decision
A good test of an agency's keenness to sell your property is to invite them to value it at 9 p.m. or 8 a.m., but since this is rather unfair and you probably do not want them around at that time, it is rare that a prospective vendor requests this. Watch for any signs of an agent not being prepared to inconvenience himself though, because this attitude is likely to be taken with all his business dealings.

Each agent should be given plenty of time to sell the services his firm has to offer. Let him look at the property (there is no point in measuring up at this stage) and then sit him down and let him give his opinion. Do not let him know the figure you are anticipating until after he has made his own clear and be wary of the agent who then adjusts his opinion to fit your own, however subtly this is done. Unless your property is something out of the ordinary, you can expect an opinion on the spot – the agent who needs to go away and think about it does not know his area. If he needs the assistance of someone else in his office, which is probably the case, why did that person not come too?

"WHY DID HIS PARTNER NOT COME TOO."

Having given his views on value, he should then extol the virtues of his firm – some of which will be relevant.

You will need to know about:

Commission Rates – For sole and multiple agency.
Advertising – Is it extra? How frequently will he advertise?
Who handles the Sale? – Will the person valuing deal with the matter all the way through? If not, you want to speak to the person who will, to find out his general attitude, especially to work in the contract stage.
Contract Stage – If he is good, he will have already clarified this – if not, find out how involved he gets.
Hours of Business – Does this include a full-time member of staff on Sundays?

Details – Colour photographs or black and white? Can you approve them before they are circulated?
For Sale Board – Is there a reduction in fees for having one?
Appointments – Will he accompany if required? Do they check reactions and report back?

It is important that you get on with the person handling the sale, if you find the agent abrasive, forget it; you may have to go through many difficult situations together and you need all the camaraderie you can get.

In order to make your decision consider:

Valuation

The three or four agents' opinions plus your own will have enabled you to arrive at a suitable asking price. The agent that gave you a wildly optimistic figure either does not know his values or is trying to gain the instruction based on your greed, in the hope that he will persuade you to take a realistic figure later. The agent who undervalued is probably too cautious for his own good, but do not dismiss him out of hand for this reason as he may handle the marketing, negotiation and after sales very well.

Commission Rates

You will probably find that these are fairly uniform. The agent who is a lot cheaper than the others is unlikely to be able to do the job properly. Commission may well be negotiable, so if the firm you really want is a bit more expensive try and get him to reduce his rate. The pillar of society mentioned earlier, is likely to be expensive and unyielding.

Advertising

This depends on where you are in the country. In some

areas you will be expected to pay, in which case make sure you retain control of how much is spent. In others it is inclusive and you should make sure that your property gets coverage for at least the first four weeks and then every other week until a sale is agreed. If the agent has confidence in his valuation there is no reason why he should not agree to this.

Who Handles the Sale?
Continuity is important – how can somebody expect to

"THE PILLAR OF SOCIETY IS UNLIKELY TO BE YIELDING.

negotiate on a client's behalf if he does not know the background and has not seen the property?

Hours of Business

Few good agents pack up and leave the office at 5.30 p.m. Their commitment is usually stronger than that. The best answer you can get is that 'closing time is 5.30 p.m. but we rarely get away before 6.30 p.m.'. Some agencies stay open until 8 p.m. these days, which is usually worthwhile. As weekends are peak viewing time, it is also desirable that your agent should be open on both these days – preferably with a full-time member of staff present, not just a casual.

Details

There is no reason why you should not approve a draft of the details before they are printed – do not be too fussy though. Try and get your agent to use colour photographs if possible as they always look better.

For Sale Board

If an agent genuinely believes that a board will help him to earn his commission there is no reason why he should not give you a reduction. Ten per cent is reasonable. You have the right to refuse one.

Appointments

If you go away for a weekend and leave a key, your agent should be willing to take people round your property. Chasing applicants for their reactions and reporting them back to you should be obligatory.

Sole or Multiple Agency?

As a rule, sole agency is cheaper and ensures a grea e commitment from the agent but in larger cities one often finds that the rates are the same for both and in these instances it might be better to give it to two or three agencies. Never have more than one board. If you do instruct a sole agent, ensure that you have the right to terminate the arrangements whenever you wish, as you may get to a point when nothing has happened and you wish to widen the field. The sole agent might suggest that he instructs other agents on what is known as a half commission basis when you say you intend to do this, but bear in mind that you will be splitting the reduced sole agency fee with him and the incentive to take proper action will be reduced. *Never grant anybody sole selling rights*, as you will be liable for commission even if your brother buys your property.

" BE SURE YOU HAVE THE RIGHT
TO TERMINATE THE
AGREEMENT. "

Consider the matter carefully once the agents have gone away and notify the successful agent of your decision, making an appointment for him to come and take details. It is a good idea to let the unsuccessful agents know that you have not opted for them, and why – it may encourage them to improve their service.

The following chapter informs you of the standard of service to expect at each stage of the transaction.

4

ESTATE AGENTS' PROCEDURE

When instructed to proceed with the marketing of a property, the agent will act at a pace which depends on the efficiency of his office and whether he is in competition with another agent.

Estate agents are obliged by law to confirm the details of commission due to them in the event that they

THE AGENT WILL ACT AT A PACE WHICH DEPENDS WHETHER HE IS IN COMPETITION.. ...OR NOT.

introduce a purchaser who proceeds to completion. If they fail to confirm instructions, they are not entitled to any commission. Similarly, if your sole agent instructs another agent on a half commission basis and the sub-agent introduces a buyer, the vendor is not liable to pay any commission unless the arrangement is confirmed in writing.

Marketing Stage

Preparation of Details
The standard of details varies enormously from one agent to another. Some maintain that they are of little or no value and restrict them to room sizes. Others reveal frustrated literary aspirations and are laughably flowery. Most fall between and serve their purpose. A good photograph is important, unless your property is one of the few that refuse to look presentable on film. This is usually followed by a description of location and local amenities, the type of property and any outstanding features. The detailed breakdown should include room sizes and any features within the room. Special care should be taken in the kitchen. Outside, garden and garage size should be mentioned. Most agents will include rates payable and in the case of leasehold property, the length of the lease, ground rent and maintenance liabilities. Do not be surprised at the speed with which your agent takes details – he will have done this many times before and have it down to a fine art – and resist the temptation to chat to him as he takes particulars as he will be distracted and might miss something.

If you wish to check a draft of the details, do not try and change their style or insert too much detail; the agent usually knows what is required. All you are looking for are glaring omissions.

Circulation of Details

When the agent returns to his office with the approved particulars they will be typed out and suitable applicants will be selected from his mailing list. Applicants are selected by a variety of methods ranging from an office junior sifting by hand cards containing prospective buyers' details to a computerised matching system. If the office junior is reasonably bright, his method, although slower, is more selective as computers will only respond to hard facts and are oblivious to the whims and fancies of applicants. The selection is always a difficult matter as agents are only too aware of those fickle applicants who buy well above or below the price range given. To be on the safe side, a property on the market at say, £60,000 may be sent to everybody looking between £45,000 and £75,000. The only certainty is that the majority will be in the bin the following day.

Selection by an office junior also makes it easier to set aside particularly suitable applicants to be telephoned. The chances are that the agent will get a couple of applicants round the same day as receiving instructions, which may impress his client enormously but most of the people contacted in this matter will just ask for details to be sent. Telephoning applicants is of debatable value to the vendor; the applicants will get the details the following day anyway. It might occasionally be the case that an applicant will be headed off by a telephone call from agreeing another deal, but this must be rare. Telephoning is more for applicants' and agents' benefit than anything else. Applicants like to see a property as early as possible if they are keen to buy and agents can build up a rapport with potential clients. An applicant is far more likely to be telephoned if he has a property the agent wants to sell because he stands to earn two commissions.

For Sale Boards
An agent will nearly always suggest that you have a board whether it is likely to help sell the property or not, because it advertises his firm.

Occasionally a buyer is introduced by a board, so unless you object strongly on aesthetic grounds, have one for as long as you can stand the sight of it. Arguments in favour of boards are stronger in areas where there is no obvious focal point for local advertising and if your property is of an unusual nature. Catch an agent off guard and he will admit that surprisingly few properties are sold as a result of an applicant seeing a board.

There is little point in letting the agent convert the board to 'Under Offer' or 'Sold Provisionally' once a buyer has been introduced unless you feel he has done very well and it is permitted by way of a reward.

Window Display
The overall impression of a window display is important to an agent's image and has a positive effect in bringing applicants with casual enquiries into his office. It is not always possible for an agent to display every property on his register in the window, although a good agent will always try to get his latest instructions in.

Only very few properties are sold in this manner and those that are will tend to be out of the ordinary.

Advertising
This is one of the major items of expenditure for an estate agent. He must be seen to advertise in the local papers, and in the case of the agents in the big cities, the evening papers. The grander London and country house agents need to be seen in the nationals.

A client has every right to see his property advertised regularly. In the period when a buyer is most likely to be introduced, which is the first four weeks, a property should be advertised each week. A good photograph is important in the locals, but quality of reproduction varies from one paper to another so do not blame your agent if it is poor. Price alone beneath a photograph is not enough so your agent will give brief details of location and accommodation. Wait for the circulation of details and the appearance of any newspaper advertising before accepting an offer so that you reach the greatest number of prospective buyers.

Prominent advertising is in the interests of both agent and vendor; it is the most likely way in which a purchaser is going to be introduced to a property and from the agent's point of view, it brings in applicants for all his properties and if he has an impressive spread, will attract potential clients. If your property has a potential specialist market as it will if it has for example, extensive stabling, then suggest to your agent that he tries an appropriate magazine – in that instance, 'Horse and Hound' is worth a try.

Appointments

The agent should make appointments and confirm them with his client, ensuring at all times that he has the name, telephone number and address of the applicant. This is for two principal reasons. One is security, in case of theft etc. The other is in order to find out what the person thought of the property. Pointless as this may initially seem, it is useful to have on record the opinions applicants have of the property and quite surprising how often people foster misconceptions with regard to schools, shopping facilities, transport etc. If you decide to take a drop in price later on in the proceedings it can also be beneficial to have a note of applicants whose only objection to your property was price.

A good agent will always accompany applicants if requested to do so, whether you are present or not. If a property is empty, even if it is unfurnished, applicants should always be accompanied.

Offer Stage

Researching Offers

This is a crucial aspect of agency work that is neglected by some. It involves the agent verifying the precise position of the applicant making the offer and that of the applicant's prospective purchaser and so on until he reaches the end of the chain. Only by doing this can an offer be seen in its true perspective.

It involves finding out the nature of the properties involved, whether surveys have been carried out, the mortgages required, expectations of time-scale, the period the transaction has been under way. He must speak to the solicitors/conveyancing companies, the agents/vendors and building societies/banks that are concerned, cross-checking claims that are made. Naturally there will be times when an agent is misled but these should be the exception. He should notify his client if there are any weak links in the chain, e.g. an unsettled divorce case (notorious for dragging matters out) or an inexperienced couple expecting a high mortgage on a property in poor condition. It is pointless to run up a large solicitor's bill whilst hoping that a crumbling chain will hold together.

Submitting Offers and Negotiating

An agent should submit all offers to his client as quickly as possible and verify details of the applicant's position. If there is more than one offer he should give both parties a good chance to make their best bid (preferably without letting either party know the other's bid), and then submit both with recommendations as to which will suit his client's situation best. Normally the agent will be impartial in this event, but the temptation to exaggerate the merits of a particular applicant arises under some circumstances. E.g. Buyer A and buyer B both submit offers that are identical. Buyer B is in a slightly better position with a shorter chain but has found a buyer for his own property through a rival agent. Buyer A has found a buyer through your agent. Doubt may be subtly cast on buyer B's intentions and buyer A's case will be boosted, as the agent will point out that he knows all about him and will be able to follow the situation closely. The actual reason will be that he does not want to lose buyer A's purchaser by making him wait around too long. Nothing outrageous but a manoeuvre that is more in your agent's interest than your own.

A client usually has a fixed idea of the price he is willing to accept but often does well to keep this to himself until the latter stages of the negotiation, as the agent may feel inclined to use that as his starting point as opposed to the asking price. Remember that there is no rule which says that you are obliged to take a figure less than your asking price, but do bear in mind that your agent will know when the applicant is nearing the end of his tether. He has taken the offer and as a result has a better insight into its flexibility and conviction.

It is surprising how many applicants when making their offer say that they will offer more if necessary, giving the agent an excellent opportunity to boost his own stock by intimating to his client that if he works hard on the fellow he might get him to go up a bit.

A common mistake is made in assuming that because an agent is on a percentage, he will try and get the best price; two per cent of £1000 is only £20. The unscrupulous agent would far rather tie up a deal than risk losing it for the sake of gaining his client an extra £1000.

If you have instructed more than one agent, you must be especially aware of the temptation to exaggerate claims made when two offers are received from separate firms. There is little an agent dislikes more than to get so near and then have a deal snatched away from him by a rival. This situation can be highly detrimental to the client's interests.

An applicant will sometimes suggest to a client that they can both save money by cutting out the estate agent. This is usually done by withdrawing the property from the market then proceeding a week or two later. Refuse point blank and have nothing more to do with this person. Not only is it dishonest to take this course, but there is a good chance that this type of person will try and cheat you at some stage of the proceedings – usually the day before exchange of contracts when you have little choice but to comply. The agent nearly always finds out about such activities and starts legal proceedings.

Sometimes a property is undervalued and everybody who sees it wants to buy. You have two courses to take if this happens. The easiest is to withdraw the property from the market and have another go at the correct price a month later. If you are in a hurry to sell, though, a good agent should be able to handle the situation. He has got to swallow his pride and admit to all applicants that the price was too low and tell them that a figure in excess is expected. He must let as many people as possible see the property and fix a date by which offers must be submitted, preferably as a sealed bid, since this appears to be fairer. They will then be considered by his client in the usual way. A bit messy but if it is carefully done, applicants will have no reason to complain. (See page 125 from the purchaser's point of view.)

An agent is sometimes given a higher offer after a sale has been agreed, laying him open to the charge of gazumping. In most cases this is unfair as an agent is only as good as the client who instructs him. As always, the agent is duty bound to submit the higher offer and if it is accepted he gets the unenviable job of telling the original proposed purchaser the bad news. This unfortunate situation arises in any agency, good or bad, but the good agent will have narrowed down the possibility of it happening by speaking to everybody who has seen the property and shown interest before advising his client to accept an offer. He should also give the original proposed purchaser the opportunity to increase his offer when the gazumper (vendor) has made his intentions clear.

Finally, do not attempt to negotiate yourself unless you have lost confidence in your agent, or are very sure of your own skills in that regard and the purchaser prefers to negotiate direct with you. You are paying for the luxury of keeping the negotiation at arms' length so let the agent do his job and earn his money. If, as is normal, you do not wish to enter into the negotiation direct, simply say to the purchaser that you prefer him to talk about that to the agent and that the agent will be acting under your instructions. This can be done firmly and politely without any offence being created.

Preliminary Deposits

Most agents will admit that preliminary deposits (paid by the purchaser to the estate agent when a sale has been agreed) are of little or no value these days – many have found that the regulations relating to the administration of clients' accounts in which deposits must be kept are too cumbersome and expensive and have given up asking for them.

Preliminary deposits are supposed to be a sign of

goodwill but since they are instantly returnable at any stage of the transaction, if somebody wants to deceive this will not stop them.

The small benefits to the agent lie in knowing when a proposed purchaser is withdrawing his offer (as he will ask for his deposit to be returned) and in knowing that if a vendor were to argue about commission, the agent will at least have some of his money in hand (even though the proposed purchaser pays the deposit the credit is usually transferred to the vendor on completion).

Purchasers are rarely keen to give money to estate agents and often complain of the loss of interest, but any interest earned does not cover administration costs.

Mortgages

If your prospective purchaser has not already arranged his mortgage, he may ask for recommendations from the agent. The larger agencies have separate mortgage departments giving them the advantage of being certain of the accuracy of any information they need. A smaller agency can either put the prospective purchaser in touch with a building society with which he has an agency (although this is done less than one might expect because there is rarely anything in it for the agent), or alternatively he might have an arrangement with a mortgage broker, insurance broker or financial adviser, whereby he gets a commission on any insurance policies taken out in the course of arranging the mortgage. This is not a bad state of affairs as the agent in unlikely to jeopardize the sale by putting the mortgage in the hands of an incompetent.

Solicitors

Once the sale is arranged, the agent will confirm the details to both parties and their respective solicitors. If asked to do so, the agent will recommend a solicitor –

again it is in his own interests to suggest an efficient firm but in this case it is very unlikely that a commission will be paid – instead the solicitor is likely to return the recommendation (if appropriate) when he is able and/or give legal advice to the firm and its principals at a reduced or zero rate.

Surveyors

The larger agencies will have a qualified surveyor on their staff – F.R.I.C.S., A.R.I.C.S., F.S.V.A., or A.S.V.A. (see page 30). The smaller agencies will have a local surveyor to recommend who they know will not be unnecessarily fussy – some are to a ridiculous extent. Again it is unlikely that a commission will be involved.

Do bear in mind that an applicant is not allowed to use the surveyor employed by the estate agent he is buying through, as this creates a conflict of interest.

Contract Stage

Many agents let the matter ride from this point, leaving it in the hands of solicitors and maintaining contact with one of them to see if contracts have been exchanged, so that he can send his account. It is at this time when it becomes obvious if an agent is good at his job. He should be asking if surveys have been carried out; if not, why not? Is somebody in the chain delaying on purpose? Once surveys have been carried out, he will be looking for mortgage offers. Sometimes a prospective purchaser will want to renegotiate as a result of a survey. The agent should assist his client all the way and if necessary obtain builders' estimates to back up his case. Keeping in touch with solicitors, he should ensure that Enquiries Before Contract are sent out and returned promptly, he will make sure Searches are applied for sooner rather than later, checking that no adverse comments were made and investigating them if they were.

Finally, when he knows the proposed purchaser's solicitor has in hand the ten (or five) per cent deposit, formal offer of mortgage, approved contract and Local Authority Search, he will liaise with all parties, agree a mutually convenient date for completion and suggest that they contact their solicitors at once, giving instructions to exchange contracts. These activities must be pursued in varying degrees up and down the chain, depending on the efficiency of the other solicitors, agents or vendors involved.

Once contracts have been exchanged the agent can send an invoice and breathe a sigh of relief; his commission is now secure, unless the purchaser fails to complete, which is very unusual. As a rule, the only other assistance given will be on completion day, when he will hand over the keys when given the instruction to do so.

Even if you have no intention of marketing your property yourself, read on. The information, especially relating to the contract stage, may prove very useful if you discover that your agent is not up to expectations and it is too late to get rid of him.

5

SELLING YOUR PROPERTY WITHOUT AN ESTATE AGENT

It is useful to go through the estate agents' procedure step-by-step, to show the best way of selling your own property. Inevitably he will have advantages at some points, but then so will you at others. At the important stages however, your chances are as good as an agent's.

The decision as to whether it is sensible to go it alone or not depends very much on the individual vendor, the time he has available, the area he lives in, market conditions and the type of property he is trying to sell.

Valuation

The valuation of residential property for resale purposes cannot be carried out on a scientific basis (as opposed to rebuilding costs for insurance purposes which can). As agents never tire of telling us, the value of a property is what a purchaser is willing to pay for it. This is true, and what you have to work out is the figure that relates closely to what applicants will expect to pay – before you start marketing. Look at the competition, at comparable properties that are on the market or have just sold. Be as objective as possible as you will be doing yourself no favours by putting your property on the market at a high price and wasting money on advertising.

A justifiable source of irritation to estate agents is the home owner who, having invited him to value his property under the pretext of wishing to sell through his firm, promptly starts marketing it himself. It is a cross that agents have had to bear for many years and there is nothing they can do about it.

The vendor who intends marketing his own property has a number of options open to him when it comes to valuation.

He can rely entirely on his own judgment. Most home owners have a good idea of the value of their property from keeping an eye on neighbours' sales and the local newspapers. This will not be enough of an idea for you to base a sale on though, so do what the agents do. If Agent A is valuing a property and Agent B has sold next door, it is common practice for Agent A to telephone Agent B and ask the approximate sale price, the condition of the property, the accommodation etc. There is no reason why you should not do the same. If you are still uncertain, but have a reasonable range of expectation e.g. between £48,000 and £52,000, you are not going to do any harm by asking for 'offers in the region of £50,000' or 'offers in excess of £50,000' if you are sure you will not accept below that figure. This avoids setting an upper limit to the price you can expect but still gives applicants a guide figure.

The next option is to ask for a formal written valuation from an estate agent. It is best to be straightforward with the agent and tell him what you are doing – ask him for a reasonable figure that your property should be marketed at. Argue with him if you think the figure given is too low or too high and listen to his justification. He will not be adverse to making adjustments to his original idea if your views are valid. For obvious reasons, most agents will try and convince you of the folly of your ways in going it alone but remember that many would do the same in your position. If you do ask for a written valuation it will be necessary to pay the agent a fee, as the moment he

commits an opinion to his notepaper he becomes liable
for that judgment: if it is grossly inaccurate and you suffer
as a result you could have recourse in the courts. It is not
unreasonable to expect to pay but the professional scale
fees are out of all proportion to the service you require.
Shop around and establish the fees in writing. This option
is more reassuring and does have the added advantage of
giving you a piece of paper to wave under an applicant's
nose if he starts griping about the price you are asking.

The final option is most relevant to a fast-moving and
therefore highly competitive area. Be totally straightforward with the local agents, telling them that you intend
trying to sell by yourself first, but inviting their opinions
on the premise that one or more of them will be instructed
if you do not succeed. A good agent will welcome any
chance to get a foot in the door and once more you will be
given dozens of reasons why you should not pursue your
chosen course, added to which they may try and tempt
you to instruct them with the promise that they have got
an applicant who will love your beautiful home. Resist
this, as the chances are that if the person exists you will
pick him up when you advertise. Any valuation obtained
in this manner will of course only be verbal and there are
likely to be discrepancies between agents.

Each valuation or comparable property is only an
opinion or a piece of information to be added to your own
views. With straightforward properties, i.e. those which
benefit from plenty of relevant comparables, it should be
possible to fix a definite asking price, but in doing so
remember that it is difficult to take an applicant's offer
over a rigid figure. For any property that is out of the
ordinary it is advisable to ask for 'offers in the region of'
or 'offers in excess of'. The flexibility these two prefixes
give you avoids the understandable resistance to offering
over a fixed asking price if you have pitched the figure too

low or have the good fortune of having more than one applicant bidding. Valuation is notional to the degree that your property is worth different prices to different people. E.g. the £5000 spent in double glazing a house will have a negative value to an applicant that finds it ugly and suffocating, but will be worth in excess of £5000 (for the saved effort) to the applicant who had intended to double-glaze his new house anyway.

In areas where property sells slowly and there is a large selection of similar properties on the market it is important to be very careful as applicants will be looking at as many as they can and will be aware that market conditions are on their side. Even a discrepancy of £1000 can cause problems under these circumstances but research should not be difficult.

"EVERY APPLICANT HAS A POINT IN NEGOTIATION BEYOND WHICH HE WILL NOT BUDGE"

Agents are frequently asked whether carpets and curtains should be included in the asking price. In spite of the fact that they are usually sold with the property, it is best not to include them but it makes sense to pitch your asking price at a level at which you would be prepared to include them if necessary. This way an offer that has been pushed as far as possible in negotiation, but still remains below the asking price, can be increased further when carpets and curtains are introduced and an offer of the asking price might be improved upon in a similar way. Every applicant has a point in negotiation beyond which he will not budge – it becomes a matter of pride. Throwing in something tangible such as carpets and curtains can make all the difference.

Valuation of carpets and curtains is difficult and depends on condition and how badly the prospective purchaser wants them but as a general rule, if they are in reasonable condition but not brand new, it is worth asking about half their replacement value.

Marketing Stage

Preparation of Details

This is well worthwhile as it will give applicants a chance to get an impression of the property before viewing. An impression that will help them relate it to their current room sizes, facilities, services etc., and see if the property is worth viewing. Details also establish what is included in the way of fixtures and fittings and give applicants something to mull over once they have left the property. Always type details and present them well. Most agents use photocopiers for mass reproduction and as they now give such a good standard of copy, there is no reason why you should not too. The example of layout given on pages 75 to 77 is used by many agents in various forms.

1. *Photograph*

A good photograph is important unless it makes your property look awful. It is likely to be the first sight an applicant is going to have of the property, so make it a good one. Take several from different angles to start with. The best will be obvious. The cheapest method of reproduction is to stick the original to the master copy of your details and photocopy the lot, but a better impression is given by making use of the miniprint service that many of the film processing shops now offer. A large number of small colour prints like this can be reproduced at a very reasonable price. Photographs of gardens and internals should be used if these features are exceptional.

2. *Description*

This should include the type of property, the condition, situation, location, amenities and services.

Type of property – Maisonette, flat, house or bungalow? If a flat or a maisonette, is it converted or purpose-built, which floor is it on? If a house or a bungalow, is it detached, semi-detached or terraced? Give the approximate age of the property. If it is pre-Victorian, is it listed?

The Condition – If the property is immaculate, say so – the licence agents allow themselves for 'good condition' applies to anything that has been reasonably well maintained but has suffered wear and tear for a year or three. 'Fair condition' usually means tatty and 'in need of work/modernisation' covers everything down from there.

It is a good idea to mention any recent work carried out of a major nature such as rewiring, replumbing, reroofing, new central heating or double glazing. Details should also mention any timber treatment or damp-proofing guarantees and recent decoration, inside or out.

THE CAVE

UNDER OFFER
"THE CAVE"
FIRST OCCUPIED 743, B.C.

"GIVE THE APPROXIMATE
AGE OF THE PROPERTY"

In the case of flats and maisonettes the same applies but will relate to the whole block or house.

The Situation – Is the property set well back from the road? Is it a quiet road? Does it overlook or back onto fields or woods? Does it have spectacular or pleasing views? Is it a particularly attractive situation in any other way? Is it in a prestigious residential area? Is the property within a conservation area?

The Location – Is the property near a railway station, a motorway, local or town centre shopping facilities? Are secondary, primary and nursery schools nearby? Swimming pools, golf courses and sports centres are worth mentioning. The old problem of one man's near is another man's far arises here, but you can get around this without misleading by walking or driving the distances involved and timing it. Fifteen minutes' walk from the station sounds a lot better than a mile from the station.

Services – It depends on where you are living as to what is worth mentioning. E.g. it is hardly worth saying you have all mains services if you live in the centre of Watford, but it is if you live on the edge of a village in the Cotswolds. There is nothing to be gained from holding anything back at this point, but if you are expecting mains drainage or gas to be connected in the near future, mention it; the applicant can check this out.

Amenities – This includes subjects such as central heating, cavity wall insulation, double glazing, luxury fitted kitchens or bathrooms, fitted bedroom furniture, jacuzzis, tennis courts, swimming pools etc.

Do not go overboard with the superlatives as an agent might or you will just appear to be conceited. There are bound to be individual points relating to your property or neighbourhood that you will want to mention, but the important thing is, keep it brief; if you hand an applicant five pages of details on a three bedroom house he won't read it all until he has bought the property.

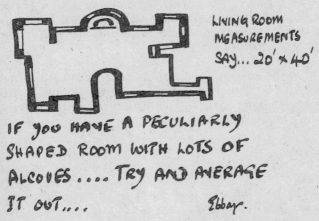

LIVING ROOM
MEASUREMENTS
SAY... 20' x 40'

IF YOU HAVE A PECULIARLY SHAPED ROOM WITH LOTS OF ALCOVES .... TRY AND AVERAGE IT OUT....   Ebbay.

3. Internal Detail

Your measurements are only meant as guidance so if you have a peculiarly shaped room with lots of alcoves, try and average it out. The best method of approaching the question of order is to start at the front door, or wherever the applicants are likely to enter the property and work your way through in the way you intend to show them when they come in person. As you look at each room be methodical in order not to miss anything – start on the floor, look at each wall and then the ceiling – familiarity can cause stupid omissions. Special care should be exercised in the kitchen as this is where the largest number

of features is likely to be located. Mention makers'
names wherever appropriate, especially with kitchen
units, bathroom suites and fitted bedroom furniture.
Counting power points used to be important but since
most houses have plenty now, it ceases to be relevant.
Similarly with radiators; if you have already said that the
property has full central heating it will be obvious that
there is a radiator in each room. If you have partial central
heating or an unusual type of central heating or double
glazing, list each feature individually.

4. *Exterior Detail*
It is worth mentioning fruit trees, vegetable plots and the
general layout of the garden. If your garden faces south or
west put this in as a feature – if not, do not. Hardstanding
and vehicular side access will be of interest to caravan and
boat owners. If you are a very keen gardener and yours is
something special, you can afford to elaborate further but
if it is pretty average, keep it simple. Communal gardens
and balconies should be treated in the same way. Always
distinguish between a double width garage and a double
length garage as applicants become irritated if you do not;
it is important to some people.

5 *Tenure, Outgoings and Price*
The tenure of a property is straightforward, either
leasehold or freehold. If in doubt, consult your solicitor.
In both cases rates payable should be mentioned (unless,
of course, the new poll tax has replaced them). With most
freehold property, rates will be the only relevant outgoing
– exceptions are when a management company deals with
the maintenance of communal areas of an estate and
when the property is located in a private road. In these
instances the annual liability should be mentioned. In the
case of leasehold property, and this includes most flats,

details of the length of lease remaining, ground rent and maintenance liability can be learned from a copy of the lease. If you do not relish the idea of wading through this document, your solicitor, who will know where to look for it, will be able to give you the information quickly. In addition to the maintenance liability, i.e. whether you pay a third, a tenth or a fiftieth of the total amount needed to maintain the property, it is worthwhile putting the amount paid for the last year. When finishing your details with the price (and incidentally with any communication

A CASTLE IN THE AIR A PROPERTY WITH A ROMANTIC PAST.

"ALWAYS ISSUE A DISCLAIMER"

relating to the property prior to exchange of contracts) it is important to put 'Subject to Contract' as a safeguard against any claim that they represent anything binding.

6. *Disclaimer*
Always include a disclaimer from any liability as a result of producing your own details. This will not excuse you from deception but does put you in the clear if somebody orders his carpets to your measurements and they turn out to be wrong by three inches.

FULL ADDRESS OF PROPERTY

VENDOR'S NAME

TELEPHONE NO.

2. *Description*
A semi-detached house built approximately fifty years ago on a generous plot in this quiet, tree-lined road. Offered in good decorative order throughout, this property has full gas central heating and is completely double glazed. The town centre, railway station and primary and secondary schools are all within walking distance.

1. Photograph

3. *The Internal Detail*
GROUND FLOOR

ENTRANCE HALL
Understairs cupboard enclosing electricity and gas meters.

LOUNGE (12′ × 12′)
Working stone fireplace with slate hearth. Fitted shelves with cupboards below.

DINING ROOM (12′ × 10′)
Fitted shelves. Serving hatch from kitchen.

KITCHEN (10′ × 8′)
Good range of fitted floor and wall units with hardwood doors. Stainless steel sink unit. Fitted shelves. Breakfast bar. Wall-mounted gas-fired boiler. Gas point. Electric cooker point. Door to garden.

FIRST FLOOR

LANDING
Airing cupboard enclosing hot water storage tank. Access to insulated loft.

BEDROOM 1 (12′ × 12′)
Double wardrobes with shelving and hanging space. Built-in dressing table.

BEDROOM 2 (12′ × 10′)
Single wardrobe with hanging space.

BEDROOM 3 (10′ × 8′)
Fitted shelves.

BATHROOM
White panelled bath with mixer tap and shower attachment. Wash basin. Medicine cabinet.

SEPARATE W.C.
White low level W.C.

4. *The Exterior Detail*

FRONT GARDEN (30′ × 40′)
Laid to lawn with flower borders. Drive with hardstanding for three cars.

GARAGE (20′ × 12′)
Lighting and power. Workbench. Fitted shelves.

REAR GARDEN (100′ × 40′)
South facing. Laid to lawn with shrub borders. Pedestrian side access.

5. *Tenure, Outgoings and Price*
RATES PAYABLE £440 for current year.

OFFERS ARE INVITED IN THE REGION OF £50,000 FREEHOLD, SUBJECT TO CONTRACT.

6. *Disclaimer*
This description is for guidance only. Accuracy is not guaranteed and it does not form part of a contract.

(Numbered headings relate to the text only. Do not include them on your actual particulars.)

Circulation of Details

The estate agent has a clear advantage here, but mainly one of speed when you bear in mind that most of his applicants have been picked up from his newspaper advertising.

If you are not yet ready to market your property and want to maximise your chances, running a preliminary announcement in the most suitable paper with a box or telephone number is not going to do any harm. Something along the lines of:

Carlton Drive, Littlehampstead. Detached house, 3 beds., 2 recep., kitchen and bathroom. Coming on the market September. Price guide £80–90,000. (If you are not sure on price yet.) Ring 000000 for early copy of details.

Security: It is best not to put the precise address in an advertisement, nor should you reveal this to anyone who rings up unless you feel happy about a particular caller. Take down their name and address and explain that the details you will send them will have all the information. This way you should avoid dealings with any unpleasant characters.

You should build up a bit of interest at an early stage and will probably end up with your own mailing list. Run the advert for two or three weeks.

Resist the temptation to dribble your house onto the market though – especially if you have yet to fix a price. Build up your list but do not show the property until you are ready – this being the point at which you are sure of your price, your particulars are ready, your advertisement is imminent and you have got your property looking the way you want it to.

For Sale Boards
As pointed out in the previous chapter, the number of
instances when a board effects a sale are few, but if you
feel strongly about it and especially if you live in an area
with poor local paper coverage, it cannot do any harm.
Undeniably there are people who cruise around areas at
weekends looking for property on the market. Most of
these will look at the paper, but take the estate agent's
attitude – you never know, it might initiate a sale. Be as
professional as possible about making your own board –
either get a signwriter to print it for you or use stencils.
The impression a very obviously home-made board gives
is not favourable. Unless you want to hold open house
while the board is up, do not put 'Apply Within'. 'Viewing
by Appointment only' and your telephone number should
put paid to this.

Window Display
If there is a well-situated Property Shop in your area, you
should consider making use of their position and placing
a photograph and details of your property with them.
They are inexpensive and should be regarded as an
advertising medium.

Newsagents' windows are a bit of a long shot at present
but the more people use them for property, the more
relevant they will become. High Street locations are
always worth a try – make sure you use a photograph.

Along similar lines, if there are two or three large local
employers in your district, try and get a friend to put a
card on the company notice board.

Advertising
This is your principal method of exposing your property
to the public. Your advertisement must be with all the
other property so choose your newspaper carefully. If

there is more than one paper with property in, it should be quite apparent which is the most relevant for yours. The likelihood is that there will be one prominent property advertiser – this is because agents dislike having to split the impact or double the cost of their advertising. You should only need to consider advertising in local papers for adjacent areas if your property is of an unusual nature.

The exceptions to weekly local advertising are in the big cities where the property goes into an evening paper such as the London Standard. Photographs are prohibitively expensive in such a paper and most advertisements are in lineage (classified), so it is not going to prejudice your position to do likewise. There are usually property features on fixed days in these papers, so make sure you research this beforehand. The nationals, especially the Sundays, are good for London and more expensive country properties. Once more, if there is a large local employer make use of this by placing an advertisement in the company magazine. Bear in mind specialist magazines if they might be relevant.

Your advertising copy should include a condensed version of the description on your details, followed by a summary of the accommodation.

The degree of abbreviation depends on your budget and personal aversion but most people would not be confused by the example opposite. Send your copy and photograph to the property advertising department asking them to ring you with a quote. If your local paper is not too expensive and you wish to make a strong impact with your first advertisement, increase the size and put in room sizes. The advert should be display (i.e. boxed) to make it stand out and look as professional as possible – always request the minimum size to take the copy provided, in order to avoid paying for a lot of blank space.

The mistake most people make when trying to sell their

For Example:

JUBILEE ROAD, EAST ELMSTEAD

Sympathetically modernised Victorian Terraced house within 3 minutes walk of Town Centre and Station. Full gas C.H. & double glazing. 3 Beds. 2 Recep. Mod. fitted kitchen. Bathroom/W.C. 60′ Garden Offers in the region of £40,000. Ring E.E. 0000 for details and appt. to view.

own property is losing their nerve; it is far more worrying to see advertisement costs going out every week than it is to think of a bill for ten times as much that you might receive in three months' time. It is crucial to retain your confidence: agents do because they know that every property sells eventually and they are used to paying for their advertising on a weekly basis – you are not. The

" IF YOU WISH TO MAKE A STRONG IMPACT WITH YOUR FIRST ADVERTISEMENT. "

doubt a vendor feels after advertising his property for three weeks without finding a buyer is an agent's greatest asset. A reassuring exercise is to work out how many advertisements you can buy for the estate agent's commission you are going to save. Difficult as it will be, you must learn to be as objective and businesslike as possible about selling your property.

It is very difficult to say how long it should take to sell a property, especially in a slow-moving area or market. The market is fickle – two identical properties can be marketed on the same day and one might take two days to

IT IS CRUCIAL TO MAINTAIN YOUR CONFIDENCE.

find a buyer, the other three weeks. Whatever the nature of the market or area, advertise every week for the first four weeks. If you have not found a buyer, look at the reactions you have had from viewings. If price is very obviously the sticking point, reduce it. In a fast-moving area you should have sold within the first four weeks, if not and you are still getting a good response to your advertising, stay with it. If viewings have tailed off, do not be afraid to take your property off the market and start again in six weeks or so when a fresh group of people is likely to be looking. In a slow-moving area, bring your advertising down to every other week and examine the situation every month.

One response that is virtually guaranteed is from the more enthusiastic of the local agents, who will be playing on your anxieties and trying to pull in an instruction. Resist them; if you have gone this far, keep your nerve and you will succeed.

Appointments

Insist that all viewing shall be by appointment. Make sure that you keep a careful note of the names, addresses and telephone numbers of every applicant. Show them round your property pointing out anything that might be of interest but was too trivial to put on the particulars. Do not try and 'hard sell' your property; applicants will back off like frightened rabbits, wondering why you feel it is necessary to do this. If you can remove any pocketable valuables without detracting from the general appearance, do so, as this allows you to invite people to wander around unaccompanied after the initial showing, giving them the chance to talk freely about any alterations they might want to make. Should you be unable to do this, beware of the couple that split up and make sure that both parties are accompanied at all times. Remember that people may bring round children that are not as well controlled as you might hope. Put any valuables that they might break out of their reach. During the gloomy months it is helpful to have photographs of your property, and its views if applicable, that were taken in Spring and Summer. As always leave as little as possible to the applicants' imagination.

Property purchase brings out the worst in a surprising number of people. Many are worried, some are nervous, some envious, many are suspicious and consequently evasive. As a result it is important to be able to remain calm and objective if people are rude. Agents are thick-skinned as a rule and have to swallow many insults to their client's properties and their profession.

When applicants are looking round your property there is no telling their real feelings. Some will enthuse continually and pronounce themselves very interested upon leaving, only to say when telephoned the next day that it is out of the question because the kitchen is far too

IF YOU CAN;

.... REMOVE ANY POCKETABLE VALUABLES !   Ebbor C

REMAIN CALM IF PEOPLE ARE RUDE.

small. Others will sneer at everything and ring up with an offer an hour later. The vendor must remain as polite as possible because goodwill is invaluable in any property transaction.

Keep a note of all viewings and make sure you ring them in a day or two for their reaction. This way you will gradually build up a general picture of applicants' impressions (there might be a recurring problem you can do something about) and make sure they are not harbouring any incorrect information about the area, facilities etc. Stress to them that you are interested in their genuine reaction and as a result you will learn a good deal about similar properties' good and bad points, which might be useful if an applicant starts making low offers and citing the other properties as examples.

Do not conceal defects. They are bound to be

discovered at some stage of the proceedings anyway and it causes a considerable amount of ill will if it becomes apparent that you have been trying to pull a fast one. Your prospective purchaser will become suspicious of everything from the tap washers to the foundations as a result. It is better to lose a proposed purchaser earlier on in the proceedings than later when you may have to write off solicitor's costs and survey fees on your proposed purchase. Defects should be pointed out and discussed openly at an early stage – people will admire your honesty and feel reassured about your demeanour during the remainder of the transaction.

Be prepared to show your property at any time, however inconvenient. If you work on the assumption that each applicant is desperate to buy, you will adopt the correct attitude.

Finally, if you are the owner of a large or noisy dog, try and keep it out of the way as it is going to distract your applicants at best and at worst it will scare the living daylights out of them, which does not create an atmosphere that is conducive to doing a deal.

Offer Stage

Researching Offers
An agent is never put on the spot by an offer – he always has to refer to his client, giving everybody time to think about it. Similarly, when you receive an offer, unless it is ridiculous, give yourself time to consider.

When you receive an offer you must start making enquiries about it straightaway in order to assess its true value. This relates to an applicant's own sale, mortgage requirements and so forth, and expectations of time scale.

The term 'cash buyer' is frequently used. It refers to an applicant who has the money instantly available, but is often used by people who have nothing to sell but do need a mortgage. If an offer is genuinely cash, then the only question you need to ask is of their expectation of time scale. It would be going too far to ask to see evidence that they have the money, so unless you are extremely suspicious of them, avoid this.

If the offer you receive is 'unencumbered' (i.e. the applicant has nothing to sell) but involves a mortgage, it is not unreasonable to ask the amount and if it is agreed in principle, i.e. that the amount requested can be justified by the purchaser's salary. Nobody can say they have a definite offer of mortgage at this point as each loan is dependent on the property it relates to and is subject to survey. Some building societies and banks now provide a Mortgage Certificate that demonstrates their willingness to lend a certain amount, which is reassuring, but of course it is still subject to survey. If this is not available, ask for the name of the bank manager, building society manager or broker who is dealing with their affairs and ask if a very large mortgage or a high proportion of the purchase price is involved. It is a good idea to ask if they mind if you speak to the relevant party to verify the figures and time scale involved. If you are uncomfortable about this, stress that it is nothing personal but that you intend taking a thoroughly businesslike approach to the matter and are only doing what you would expect an agent to do for you, were you employing one, and offer him the same information relating to your own purchase if and when applicable. If you meet resistance from the bank, building society or broker, point this out as well, adding that they are doing their client no favours by withholding information. Remember that his time and money are going to be wasted if the application is unreasonable. When you are happy about the unencumbered applicant's mortgage and expectation of time scale, you have all the information you should need. Company bridging loans are easily verified by asking for the name of the person dealing with the matter w'thin the firm.

If you are shy about direct questioning, you can ask your solicitor to ask the applicant's solicitor to determine his financial status. Discreetly done this way, potential snags, especially about time scale come to light before you find yourself with problems, or having someone back out on you.

Should your interested applicant have a property to sell, you need to make enquiries about that situation in addition to mortgage and expectation of time scale. The chain is incomplete if the property is unsold and you should ask the vendor or his agent about the viewing rate, price, nature of the property, saleability, and how long it has been on the market. The agent or vendor should be straightforward but if you suspect that they are not then an enquiry with another local agent as to price and saleability will clarify matters. If your applicant has found a proposed purchaser, then you should go through the same procedure with him or his agent as you have done with the applicant and so on down the chain until you reach the unencumbered or cash buyer where it ends. At this stage of the proceedings it is as well to check each link in detail – as a result you will get to know the vendors and agents who are optimistic, slap-dash or reliable in their claims and where to expect trouble if a delay occurs. Keep a record of claims made as you may need to refer back to them at a later stage. It is helpful to draw up a 'picture of the chain' to put the matter into perspective. In the example overleaf, you are described as OUR VENDOR for the purposes of the illustration.

From this example we can see that Mr A looks all right. Miss B has really got on with it and looks good but Mr C's building society survey has taken three weeks to arrange and he has yet to decide on a House Buyers Report or Full Structural Survey. The building society survey might have taken so long because he is going for a high percentage of the purchase price on a mortgage and is shopping around but, especially bearing in mind the type of property he is buying, he should be pushed to get his House Buyers Report or Structural Survey carried out.

This chain looks O.K. from the point of view of time scale but if Mr A's offer is acceptable you would have to get going and find a property as soon as possible.

Beware of nebulous claims such as expectations of

As of 21st March

OUR VENDOR selling to ⟶ **Mr A selling to** ⟶ **Miss B selling to** ⟶ **Mr C (first-time buyer)**

OUR VENDOR selling to and hoping to buy a £70,000 Edwardian Semi-Detached house.

Buying OUR VENDOR's prop. 30's built Semi. for £55,000 to £57,000.

Agreed 7/3 to buy Mr A's prop. Modern Terrace.

Agreed 1/3 to buy Miss B's prop. Modernised Vic. Terrace.

Awaiting Mr A's draft contract. House Buyers Report carried out, no probs. Requires mort. £15,000 (only awaiting written mortgage offer) towards purchase price from Mr A £40,000.

Draft contract from Miss B in hand. House Buyers Report or Full Struct. Survey to be decided; however, requires mort. £27,000. Date booked with surveyor 28/3. Purchase price £31,000 from Miss B.

Requires mort. £20,000 (agreed in principle).

T/Scale: May/June.

T/Scale: May, but prefers June.

T/Scale: May-June if nec

funds from a legacy, private bridging loans (few people are able to arrange this – banks are understandably reluctant to oblige) and tread carefully where a sale or purchase is dependent on a divorce settlement as delay is often used as a lever.

If you really do not want to get involved in offer research, it is not unreasonable to ask your solicitor to get involved (as stated on page 88). Obviously he will charge for his time, but he will be reliable and unbiased.

Negotiating

Give yourself time to consider each offer you receive, but do not take a week as the chances are that your applicant will doubt your commitment to the transaction – he is in a buying mood and will start looking at other properties.

The conviction and flexibility of an offer can only be judged by the person receiving it, but it is fair to say that as a rule, a first offer is an opening bid to test the ground. Most experienced agents will recommend rejection on principle. An offer's true value can only be judged when it has been properly researched. Once this has been done, you must decide its minimum value to you and proceed accordingly. Remember that every extra link in a chain increases the chance of a sale falling through and the object of the exercise is to move, not boost your solicitor's fee income. A thousand pounds conceded to pull in an unencumbered purchaser can be recouped because you are in a good position when offering on a property you want.

If you receive an acceptable offer from an applicant who has not completed his chain and you like and trust him, do not think you are being soft in giving him a chance to sell his own property. Set a reasonable period of time, say three weeks, for him to sell and then remarket your own at the end of it. Do not be talked into extending the period though. You should expect a slightly higher price for making this concession. You must use your own judgment as to how far an applicant will go – once more, confidence in your convictions is crucial and it does no harm to undermine his a little; point out the weak links in his chain, cite prices obtained for similar properties, point out the excellent value for money that your property represents and how many people are still looking at it. The applicant will be playing the same game so parry his arguments. If he says that this property or that one is cheaper, an expression of surprise that he does not buy one of them should keep him quiet – if he says it is sold, you might feel tempted to suggest either that it was undervalued or that prices have moved on since then. An argument you will almost certainly encounter when bypassing estate agents (and consequently their fees) is that the saving made enables you to sell at a correspondingly lower price. Although this may be true in theory, remember that your choice of this course has not altered the value of your property and you are not doing all the work of an estate agent in order to give your purchaser the benefit.

A further inducement to nudge the applicant along is to proffer the carrot of taking your property off the market. He will be constantly worried during the negotiation period that somebody will better his offer and you will be giving him a quick way out of his misery, even if it will cost him a little. Having said that, once you have accepted a firm offer that you have checked out properly and have proceeded to the contract stage, you would be well advised to take your property off the market for a variety of reasons. One is to be fair to your proposed purchaser and in being so, you encourage him and create the right atmosphere for your sale. In continuing to market your property once you have a proposed purchaser, you are almost certain to do so half-heartedly. Your enthusiasm for the job will diminish and if you do lose your proposed purchaser you lose the advantage of your property appearing fresh on the market to many new applicants – they will mostly know of it as being the property belonging to that untrustworthy fellow who already has a buyer.

At all times hold your cards close to your chest. Try and stay as vague as possible about the figure you will accept – lead your applicant gently but firmly on – just because you have set yourself a minimum price for acceptance, there is no need to grab the offer the moment it equals the figure. When it does however, ensure that you have spoken to everybody that has seen your property in order to reduce the chances of a better offer appearing at a later stage. Let everybody know that you are on the verge of accepting an offer; it is surprising how often this brings results – applicants invariably want something somebody else is after. (See below for the procedure if you get another offer.)

Inevitably every negotiation has its sticking point. This is when you bring any extras such as carpets and curtains into play. Quite often a few hundred pounds can be added to your price in this way. When considering carpets and curtains, it is as well to bear in mind the Stamp Duty threshold. If you are selling your property for £30,500 and this includes £700 worth of carpets and curtains, this should be stated on the contract, thereby saving your proposed purchaser £300. There is no point in paying unnecessary tax. (At the time of writing the threshold for this tax is £30,000.)

If you receive more than one offer you must be very careful to avoid being unfair to any of the parties involved, but must ensure that you take full advantage and get the best price. Research all your offers in the usual way – tell each applicant how many other people are interested and ask them to consider the matter very carefully and submit their best and final offer. It is a good idea to set a closing date to hurry along any ditherers and reassure the parties that you will not be bargaining back and forth in order to get them to push each other's offers up. Under these terms most people will submit their offer on the last day. It is worth bearing in mind the pressure you are going to put people under in these circumstances – they will not want to lose your property, but will be terrified of offering too much. Explain that they must offer the maximum it is worth to them, then they will not feel sorry if somebody else outbids them. There will be a strong temptation to give hints as some applicants will try to pressurise you. If you do, by mistake or on purpose, make sure you play fair and tell everybody who is interested. Once your deadline has expired examine all your offers carefully. The best offer should be quite clear, but if there are two of equal merit use your own judgment of the personalities involved. Tell all parties of your decision as soon as possible. Let the runner-up know that he will be the first to know if any problems arise. Handled well, this situation can result in a speedy transaction at an excellent price. Handled badly, you will find yourself the subject of much abuse and wading through an unpleasant and prolonged transaction. If you are worried by the process, your solicitor will be able to look at the matter objectively and advise you.

Occasionally a solicitor will suggest that a vendor goes with more than one proposed purchaser and begins a contract race. All parties involved have to be informed of the others' interest under the rules of the Law Society. The pressure and ill-will generated by contract races is tremendous – not only will the proposed purchasers be very emotional in their desire to buy your property, but they will also be spending money that they might lose. The uncertainty over a period of weeks upsets the most stable household and in many cases the pressure becomes too much and one or both of the proposed purchasers talk themselves out of wanting the property. The fair-minded vendor, when pursuing this course will reimburse the unsuccessful party's costs.

If you receive a higher offer after you have accepted another, you are placed in a very difficult position. Gazumping causes mistrust and ill-will. Morally it is wrong – legally the 'gazumped' party has no comeback, revealing a major flaw in our system. It is a sad reflection on our times that few people have not got their price, so if yours is offered and you are compelled to ignore your moral values, at least you can proceed as fairly as possible. You must give your original proposed purchaser the chance to equal the new offer. In nine cases out of ten he will not, even if he is able as his pride will prevent him. You could arrange to pay the original agreed purchaser's costs without prejudice. If you have gone ahead with the gazumper, be very careful. He is not the type of person to be trusted and he will feel the same about you. He is the type to try and beat you down on price the day before exchange of contracts, when to pull out of the transaction will be heartbreaking and expensive. He will probably not care about you as you did not care about your previous proposed purchaser.

To sum up on negotiation, confidence in your position is vital. Applicants will run rings around you if you appear to be desperate. Keep your integrity and credibility intact; you will need them during the contract stage.

Preliminary Deposits
Do not suggest a preliminary deposit as it causes more

trouble than it is worth. It has to be kept in a solicitor's special Client's Account by law, and is returnable upon request anyway.

Mortgages, Solicitors and Surveyors

There is no reason why you should not recommend mortgage brokers, solicitors and surveyors to your proposed purchaser. If you are aware of one that is particularly good in your area, suggest he gets a quote. Speaking to friends and neighbours to see how they fared will be of use. Alternatively your solicitor will be happy to assist, even with the recommendation of another solicitor. You might suggest another solicitor within the same firm as your own which, although it sounds a little dubious, is quite legal and a marvellous way of speeding up the transaction.

Contract Stage

Remember at all times that delay increases the risk of a fall-through.

Once an offer has been agreed, solicitors must be put in touch. Most agents type an information sheet giving the names, addresses and telephone numbers of the vendor and proposed purchaser and their respective solicitors, price agreed, mortgage required and source. It is a good idea to add to this a 'picture of the chain' to give everybody as much information as possible. In all communications, state that the transaction is still subject to contract. It should be pointed out that your buyer's and vendor's solicitors are not allowed to speak to you directly under Law Society rules, so any enquiries you wish to make of them should be directed through your solicitor.

Send your information sheets to the other three parties, and the solicitors will start the proceedings. Unless you

"REMEMBER AT ALL TIMES THAT DELAY
INCREASES THE RISK OF A FALL THROUGH"

have alternative accommodation, do not proceed at full pace on your sale until you have found a property to buy which is ready for sale so that the chain is complete.

Coping with Chains
Many chains are trouble-free and the transactions go without a hitch, but if you are going to deal with your own sale it is important to have the knowledge to deal with problems or delays that might occur.

Here is a picture of the chain again – using the same examples as in 'Researching Offers' on page 90.

As of 7th April

Mr Y selling to ⟶ Mrs Z selling to ⟶ OUR VENDOR selling to ⟶

Mr Y selling to	Mrs Z selling to	OUR VENDOR selling to
Buying new house – building is on schedule – agreed 28/3.	agreed 4/4 to buy Mr Y's house built 3 yrs ago (still under N.H.B.C. Guarantee).	agreed 6/4 to buy Mrs Z's house, an extended Edwardian Semi-Detached.
	Awaits draft contract.	
Has paid deposit on builder's contract. Mort. £30,000 (agreed in principle. Mort. survey booked 8/4. Purchase price £110,000.	Mort. £25,000 (agreed in princ.). (About to arrange survey.) Purchase price £80,000.	Mort. £25,000 (agreed in princ.). Purchase price £70,000. (Told own solicitor to send out draft contract for own sale to Mr A straightaway.)
T/Scale: 1st week in June earliest.	T/Scale: June/July (is on holiday 15/6 to 29/6).	T/Scale: As soon as possible.

Mr A selling to →	Miss B selling to →	Mr C
agreed 21/3 to buy OUR VENDOR's Property 30's built Semi.	agreed 7/3 to buy Mr A's Property Modern Terrace.	agreed 1/3 to buy Miss B's Modernised Vic. Terrace.
Mort. £20,000 (agreed in princ.).	Mort. £15,000 (offer now in hand).	Mort. £27,000.
(Survey & House Buyers Report booked 8/4.)	No probs. with House Buyers Report.	House Buyers Report on 28/3 revealed roof probs. Builders estimating. Deal could be in balance unless negotiation resolves. with firm mort. offer made possible.
Is awaiting OUR VENDOR's draft contract. Purchase price £56,000.	Draft contract OK'd between both solicitors. Purchase price £40,000.	No comment on draft contract. Purchase price £31,000.
T/Scale: May/June.	T/Scale: May. but prefers June.	T/Scale: May – but June if necessary.

Mr Y looks good as long as the builder stays on schedule. Builders instruct their agents (whether 'in house' or an outside firm) to be very rigorous in their research of chains, as time is money in their business so in this instance they are likely to be aware that if Mr Y's house is not finished by the middle of June, completion is not going to be possible until the end of the month at the earliest because of Mrs Z's holiday, thereby jeopardising the stability of the end of the chain (Mr C and Miss B are unlikely to be happy if the matter drifts into July). Make sure that they have noticed this. Although the efficiency of the builder's agent is an advantage in most cases, it should be remembered that the builder is the only one in the chain looking for a profit so if he starts giving deadlines for remarketing his property owing to a delay, you can assume that he means it. Sometimes such ruthlessness can mean the difference between a profit and a loss on a project.

Mrs Z looks O.K. although she is being a nuisance by going on holiday at such an important time (it is a good idea to ask everybody in the chain if they have any holiday plans especially if you find yourself moving in this summer holiday period). Mr Y's property should not throw up any problems on survey, as it is only three years old. It is still covered by the National House Builders Council guarantee if anything should turn up (this guarantee is valid to a diminishing extent over a ten year period). However, if Mrs Z does not receive a draft contract from Mr Y within two weeks then Mr Y and/or his solicitor's efficiency are suspect and you need to make sure Mrs Z presses her solicitor to chase up Mr Y's draft contract. Mr Y could turn out to be a ditherer who will eventually change his mind even though he may lose his deposit.

OUR VENDOR should feel comfortable about his own

position or he would not be proceeding, however, bearing in mind that the property he wishes to purchase is about eighty years old and is likely to have some defects, he would be wise to have his survey carried out as soon as possible. The fact that the property has been extended should be watched carefully too. He should ask his solicitor to verify as soon as possible that the extension has the correct planning permission and that the appropriate building regulations were adhered to. If they have not, his solicitor will advise him to find another property.

Mr A has been a little slow in submitting his mortgage application and thereby getting our vendor's property surveyed, but this is understandable as the chain was not yet complete.

Miss B is the most advanced on her purchase, already having her mortgage offer but her sale does not look so good.

It is unlikely that Mr C has any flexibility financially and if the builders' estimates are too high he may have to drop out. Mr C is the weakest link and should be watched carefully.

This gives a complete view of the situation and highlights the areas to watch. Readers may notice that Mr Y took a gamble when he agreed to buy his new house which was already being built, that he would be able to sell and have the money ready to pay for it. Perhaps he is a rich man or has bridging facilities available should the need arise. Mrs Z also appeared to gamble for a couple of days (perhaps it was a weekend) before she knew that her own sale was agreed to OUR VENDOR. She may not have known that it is best to wait until one has a buyer for one's own sale before agreeing to buy another property (even though matters are still subject to contract). A lot of people don't worry too much and some inevitably get

away with it.

In the first couple of days it is worth speaking to everybody in the chain and making sure they have instructed their solicitors; it is often the case that people think they can afford to wait a week or two before doing so. Fear of losing money and ignorance are two hurdles it may be necessary to overcome during the contract stage, so be patient and courteous at all times. As an example, occasionally a proposed purchaser will get it into his head that he should not apply for his mortgage until his solicitor says the contract is satisfactory. Pointing out that this action (or lack of it) is likely to delay and jeopardise the purchase and thereby put at great risk the fees he will incur from his solicitor, should put him right – if you do get one of these in your chain 'hold his hand' all the way.

Everyone in the chain should have instructed for Searches to be carried out by now. Councils are taking so long these days it may already be a little late to be sure they will be completed in time for the exchange of contracts to take place. (No solicitor should allow you to exchange contracts until it is known there are no problems arising from the Searches.)

A weekly routine check up and down the chain will keep you in touch with events without pestering people unnecessarily. You will be able to gauge if people are proceeding sluggishly or not by comparing their progress with that of your own sale and purchase. It may be necessary to speak to some parties more frequently than weekly if the situation does not look good, as in the case of Mr C. Overleaf is our example three weeks later.

Mr Y has moved on fast as the builder wants an early exchange of contracts. Once he has his Search he will be ready to exchange. Mrs Z took rather a long time to submit her mortgage application and therefore get the survey carried out, but the formal offer of mortgage should not be long in coming through. As expected with OUR VENDOR's purchase, questions arose in connection with the planning permission: following an inspection by the Local Authority, a document is awaited. The survey raised a few problems but nothing one should not expect in an eighty-year-old house. Mr A is ready to exchange but has renegotiated the price as the survey revealed damp that will cost £300 to remedy. Even though one should initially resist any price reduction, it is not unreasonable to concede on a point such as this as the proposed purchaser cannot possibly have been expected to notice it during his viewings that led to the offer.

To return to the example about three weeks later:

As of 1st May

Mr Y selling to ──────→ Mrs Z selling to ──────→ OUR VENDOR selling to ──────→

Mr Y selling to	Mrs Z selling to	OUR VENDOR selling to
agreed 28/3 to buy new house.	agreed 4/4 to buy Mr Y's 3 yr old house.	agreed 6/4 to buy Mrs Z's house.
Mort. £30,000 (offer in hand).	Mort. £25,000 (surveyed 20/4). Mort. offer expected 7-14 days. House Buyers Report O.K.	Mort. £25,000 (surveyed 19/4). Mort. offer expected any day. Survey apprvd.
Purchase price £110,000.	Purchase price £80,000.	Purchase price £70,000.
T/Scale: 1st week in June earliest. Building on schedule. Contract approved. Search due any day.	T/Scale: June/July (is on holiday 15/6 to 29/6). Minor points in contract now received, still to approve. Search in hand, revealing nothing to worry about. this being confirmed by Mrs Z.	T/Scale: As soon as possible. Contract O.K. Minor points on planning permission to verify. Search due in a week.

Mr A selling to ⟶ **Miss B selling to** ⟶ **Mr C**

Mr A selling to	Miss B selling to	Mr C
agreed 21/3 to buy our Semi.	agreed 7/3 to buy Mr A's house.	agreed 1/3 to buy from Miss B.
Mort. £20,000 (offer in hand).	Mort. £15,000 (offer in hand).	Mort. £27,000 (approved subject to a retention of £1,500 until roof is repaired).
Purchase price £55,700 (re-negotiated after survey revealed a small gutter problem causing damp internally).	Purchase price £40,000.	Purchase price £31,000.
T/Scale: May/June. Contract approved. Search in hand. *Ready to Exchange.*	T/Scale: May pref. June. Contract approved. Search in hand. *Ready to Exchange.*	T/Scale: May/June. Contract approved. Search in hand. Shortfall of £1,200.

Miss B is ready to exchange on her purchase but is having problems on her sale. Mr C, upon learning that the property needed £1200 worth of work on the roof (the discrepancy between the quote and the retention is not unusual), was confident he could borrow the money from relatives, but failed. As a result the whole chain is in jeopardy for the sake of £1200. Since Mr C is a first-time buyer, he is unlikely to take the initiative, so if matters seem to be drifting it is up to you. Firstly you must speak to Miss B who, in theory, should make up the shortfall, but her finances only allow her to make a concession of £500, which leaves £700 still needed.

Find out if Mr C is buying any fixtures or fittings, carpet or curtains. Let us suppose here that he is – some carpets to the value of about £200. This will be useful.

Next go to the other vendors. Explain the situation to them. As OUR VENDOR, let us assume you are willing to make a concession of £100. Mr Y, Mr Z and Mr A agree likewise (a small amount for avoiding a fall through). Mr C's purchase price has now been reduced from £31,000 to £30,100, and only £300 is still needed.

Since he is buying carpets to the value of £200, the contract price can be put at £29,900, thereby saving him £300 in Stamp Duty (which at the time of writing does not apply to contracts below £30,000). He will now be in a position to proceed, having gained concessions of the full £1200 required to bring the roof up to standard. £500 from Miss B, £400 from the others in the chain and £300 Stamp Duty. Mr C will still have to find £1500 for the period between completion and having the work on the roof carried out, but he should have no problem finding a short-term bank loan to cover that period.

Most people are sensible and see the logic in reducing the price of their property by a small amount if the circumstances are carefully explained. If you meet resistance or the shortfall is too great to cover, remember that some agents will see the sense in reducing their fees to make sure the sale goes through, reluctant as they may be. Always get confirmation in writing of any fee reduction.

Ten days later everyone in this example in the chain has in hand their Search, mortgage offer and an approved contract.

There is often an unnecessary lull in the proceedings at this point but it is no time to relax. Solicitors tend to write to their clients asking them for their instructions regarding a completion date. Up to a week can be saved if one party gets onto the telephone and pinpoints a date, suggesting that the others ring up their solicitors with the instructions and, if they have not already done so, for an appointment to sign the contract and hand over the deposit. The commonest period between exchange and completion is 28 days, but there is no reason if the parties are willing and able, why it should not be more or less. In this instance, an exchange on 14th May with completion on 11th June gives everybody plenty of breathing space and fits in with their plans. The exchanges should take place by telephone between the solicitors, which is customary, starting with Mr C as solicitors will not exchange on a purchase until they have already exchanged on the sale. The transaction is now firm – start packing and transferring gas, electricity, telephone, etc. Remember you must insure your purchased property from this point (see page 129).

Had Mrs Z's holiday got in the way of the completion date that most people wanted, she could have completed early by borrowing the money from the bank – they are quite amenable to this once exchange has taken place (but it is essential to talk the possibility through before exchange, to be sure you know where you stand) and it is not outrageously expensive – 90% of £80,000 is £72,000. If she borrows at say 15% this will cost less than £30 per day. If this had happened, of course, Mr Y would also be able to move early.

Transfers have to be signed, mortgage monies brought to hand and estate agents' fee notes approved once exchange has taken place, and on completion day the transfer of funds will begin with Mr C again – the money he pays to Miss B enables her to complete with Mr A and so on. This is all done very swiftly these days by computer transfer. If completion dates are different and you are running a bridging loan, then, with large amounts involved it will be worth your while agreeing with your solicitor to transfer the completion money due to you, direct to your bank by the same system instantly he receives it; you may be charged a few pounds for doing this but it's a lot cheaper than paying an unnecessary day's interest.

Never release the keys of your property until your solicitor has given you the go-ahead – he will not do this until the completion money is in hand.

Removal Firms
It is best to compare estimates and services as a prelude to making your decision to move. When you have made your choice, book them provisionally once exchange is imminent and confirm it once exchange has taken place. If you are aiming for a Friday completion, make your provisional booking as early as possible as this is their busiest day. Make sure the removal firm includes transit/storage insurance to your satisfaction.

When Not to sell Your own Property
There are circumstances when one would be ill-advised to attempt to sell one's own property.

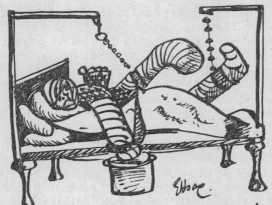

"THERE ARE CIRCUMSTANCES WHEN ONE WOULD BE ILL ADVISED TO ATTEMPT TO SELL ONE'S OWN PROPERTY"

It is a process that needs to be taken very seriously so if you are only half-hearted or you do not think you will have the time – use an agent.

Expensive and unusual country and city property requires very careful handling and mistakes will cost a great deal of money – use an agent.

Finally, if the property market is particularly inactive you can waste an awful lot of money to no avail on advertising – use an agent.

Summary
Be fair, be confident, be methodical and you should make

your move as smooth as possible. Having read what is involved in selling your own property, you may now feel that agents deserve every penny they get. A good one often does. The fees can be saved through your own endeavours though. You have an advantage over agents in that applicants think they are going to save on agents' fees by buying direct – they will discover that this is not the case when they start negotiating, but by that time you have got them.

Another encouraging point to note is the number of builders, whose livelihoods depend on selling property, that sell their own these days and many of those who do use agents are only doing so because the agent introduced the land to them and it is recognised form that in repayment for finding a site, the agent gets to sell the properties built on it.

6

WHO NEEDS AN ESTATE AGENT WHEN BUYING PROPERTY?

The short answer to this question is that the majority of people do, but there is a right and a wrong way to deal with them and it is worth pointing out a few misconceptions and pitfalls. It can only assist you if your approach helps the agent to do his job better. Additional aspects, such as auctions, new property, private sales and dilapidated property must also be considered. But first:

Examine Your Motives – Is it Worth the Extra Money and Effort?
As any property transaction is potentially difficult it is crucial that you consider the matter very carefully at all stages of the proceedings. This may sound obvious but it is surprising how many people withdraw from a deal halfway through the contract stage because they have been thinking it over and it does not seem worthwhile. You can save yourself an awful lot of effort and, in the later stages, money by examining and re-examining your motives. These may be a need for an extra bedroom or reception room, a larger garden or a garage, perhaps a change from a purpose-built flat to a conversion with more character, or from a terraced house to a semi-detached, or, later on in life, from a larger detached to a more manageable bungalow. Maybe you want to move to a better area or close to your workplace or the

children's schools. The compulsive D.I.Y. enthusiast will often want to move once he has nothing left to do on his current property. An increasingly apparent reason over the last few years has been the desire to move just because one can afford to or in order to take advantage of the tax relief.

Whatever your motives, make sure they are strong enough to warrant a few months living in that uncomfortable state of limbo that is almost inevitable when moving house in England and Wales.

Once your motives are clear it is important to come down to earth and look at your financial position as suggested in Chapter 2 'Before you Sell'. This is unlikely to be precise but you will be able to get a good idea of the price range you can afford. Do bear in mind though, moving expenses are not where it ends; a larger property means larger bills – rates, gas/oil, electricity, possibly new carpets and curtains and almost certainly new furniture.

Your Requirements
Consider your motives for moving and compare your current accommodation with the type of property you hope to purchase, although it is worth examining your current situation carefully for facilities you are indifferent to in order to make the realisation of your hopes easier. Make a list of the essentials and work from that. You may find that you will compromise later but consider the implications carefully before you do. On a Spring day it may seem worthwhile putting up with a small house for the sake of that wonderful view and spectacularly large garden but remember that you are going to have the children constantly under your feet during the long Winter. It is impossible not to get emotionally involved when buying the property you

intend to live in but do not let it carry you away.

Having decided upon the type of property you want and how much you can afford the time has come for action, but do check in the local paper that your requirements are not way beyond your price range and save yourself possible embarrassment. Estate agents can be infuriatingly condescending to the wildly optimistic applicant.

Finding the Home You Really Want

It is important to spread your net as widely as possible so start by putting your name on every agent's list in the area – even when dealing with one of the networks of computer-linked independent small agents, as they quite often have 'exclusive' instructions. Do not assume that agents advertise every property in the newspapers; some of the older style agents are too stingy and those dealing with hundreds of properties do not have room. Also, some properties may already be under offer by the time they are advertised in the newspapers.

Visit the estate agents' offices if possible, especially if you are moving locally; the way that you see properties being presented to you is the way yours will be dealt with if you chose to employ that agent. In any event a visit helps to show you the more active and enthusiastic offices and individuals – those worth keeping in close touch with.

When giving estate agents your requirements you may be surprised how little information they require. There is little point in trying to impress on them that you must have a south-facing garden or hate pebble dash and plastic baths. Price range, type and age of property, number of bedrooms and reception rooms and area are the basics. This is principally because applicant-filing-systems are usually computerised to one extent or another these days. It is usually only the old fashioned system of an office junior sorting cards by hand that will be able to cope with anything but basic requirements. As a result of the current systems you will inevitably receive an awful lot of information you are not interested in, not to mention cards asking you if you wish to stay on the mailing list only four days after you went on it. Try not to be annoyed about this – it's their problem.

Whilst in the estate agent's office you may see your ideal property displayed with an 'under offer' slip on it. Do not hesitate to make enquiries about it and if it still sounds good, ask for your name to be put on file in case it falls through.

It cannot be stressed too strongly that you must remember at all times that the agent, charming as he may be, is working for the vendors and only makes money by making a sale. For this reason one must never tell an agent precisely the highest price you can go to. Remember that if you buy through this agent, you will be negotiating against him. He might, quite reasonably, ask about your mortgage and in these days of increasing involvement of financial institutions offer to assist even if you do not buy through him. This is a relatively recent source of income for agents. As it is worth shopping around, see what he has to offer.

You may feel it is worthwhile viewing a couple of properties at this stage. Not a bad idea as it will help you to get used to the methods of description and put the price you are able to pay into better perspective. As well as viewing or telephoning the estate agents, make sure that you scan the newspapers for private advertisements and new developments (if relevant).

You might wish to take matters a stage further and actively canvass properties you think might be suitable – estate agents do this, often on a more random basis so why shouldn't you? Be fair though. If a property has an agent's board outside, give him a ring. Keep any such canvassing letter short and polite:

Dear Sir/Madam,

I am currently seeking a property to purchase in this area and from the outside yours looks as if it may be suitable. Should you be thinking of moving, I would be very grateful if you would let me know so that we may discuss the matter further – the obvious mutual advantage would be in the saving of estate agents' fees.

If you are not considering a move, please forgive me for troubling you.

Yours faithfully,

Along similar lines, a card in a newsagent's window or on a company notice board stating your requirements might secure a private sale. A long shot but it has been known to work.

After your first foray you should have a large quantity of particulars to consider. From here on it should be a steady flow, but in the meantime you have to sort through what you have got. The reason for the great volume at first is that you are not only getting the week's new instructions but also the 'Turkeys' that have been languishing on the market for three, six or even nine months. Some may have been overpriced at first, but time and a rising market may have made up the difference Some will look remarkably good value at first and only when you go to view and discover the petrol station/cement works/airport/sewage works next door do you discover why. Naturally an agent is not going to point out any of these delights on the details so you must learn to ask the right questions when making an appointment to view. This is particularly important if it involves a 100 mile round trip. Such properties are usually bought by people who had no expectation of buying anything so large and are prepared to put up with the relevant inconvenience to attain it. Under no circumstances should you buy a property of this kind if you are likely to want to move again in a hurry.

It is important at this stage of the proceedings to put in a fair bit of groundwork which involves looking at the outside of as many of the properties as possible and getting to know the locations of schools, shopping and transport facilities. This way you will quickly discover the areas you like and can afford. If you are thorough at this point you will save yourself a lot of wasted trips at a later stage.

Once you have sorted through the 'first wave' including the backlog of properties, look at your motives again – do they still seem attainable? If you have doubts it might be a good idea to forget the whole thing. If the answer is yes then it is quite probable that this is the time to get your own property on the market. Do not wait until you have lost a property through not having found a buyer on your own. The pros and cons of this decision are discussed in 'Before you Sell' under 'Sell First or Buy First?' on page 20.

You may have found the ideal property in the first wave in which case look at as many properties as you can as quickly as possible in order to compare values. If it still feels right, go for it. Every agent has heard the comment 'we love the house, but have only just started looking so cannot decide yet' and a few weeks later, 'if only we had gone for that house we saw first'. There is no need to make finding a property harder work than necessary.

Most people have to push on however, which means

getting hold of your local papers as early as possible to catch anything new on the market. Keep an eye on the nationals and Sundays too, as a few private vendors consider it worthwhile advertising there.

You must also keep in touch with the agents, especially in a very active market – this is where those visits to the offices come in useful. You will have a contact and a sense of priority as to who is most worth keeping in touch with. Unless the market is frantic, a weekly call should be enough. Some agencies will try and ring you when a new property comes in, especially if you have a property to sell in their area.

As your search continues you will become increasingly adept at sifting out the few properties worth viewing, thereby saving a lot of pointless and increasingly irritating trips. You will not reach this happy state without doing the initial groundwork, so get that out of the way as soon as possible.

Viewing Property
Some people love it, some hate it, but whatever your own feelings, however many properties you have trailed round that day, remember that this is the vendor's home and respect his feelings.

If you have made an appointment, stick to it unless you have an extremely good reason for not doing so. This basic consideration is important in maintaining general goodwill in the property market and if you do not show up it may backfire on you if ever you need the co-operation of the owner or his agent in the future. Even if you get to the outside of the property and do not like the look of it, pop in and tell the owner, truthfully but tactfully that it is not for you. Consider that every vendor who wants to show you his property has stayed in for that purpose and you will adopt the right attitude.

Assuming you like the area and are happy with the look of the outside, you will then be shown around by the owner and/or his agent. The ideal way to look at a property is unaccompanied, but few people are unwise enough to allow applicants to do this. The owner will probably talk more than the agent, knowing more detail about the property and his well-meaning banter is likely to be somewhat obtrusive. The agent will point out features and be listening to your observations, knowing that he can learn more that way. There is a tendency among a few applicants to mislead the owner into thinking they are very keen on a property when they are not, perhaps to avoid hurting their feelings. This is as pointless as it is inconsiderate – as with all property matters, honesty saves time. If you do not like the property and the owner asks why – tell him, politely.

When you have had your first look and if you are still interested, go around the property again during this first visit, hopefully on your own this time or at least with nothing to interrupt your thoughts. You have got a lot to take in over a short period. Make notes of points you will have to check; will your three piece suite fit into the living room? Will your washing machine fit in the kitchen? Will your dining table fit and so on. Most owners will be quiet if they see you scribbling and it is the only way you will remember everything.

Once you have been around the second time it is time to go, telling the owner that you are interested (if that is the case) but have many points to consider. As you leave have another look at the area – are all the facilities close enough? Will you fit in? (A young couple buying a bungalow in an area populated by over 60's also in bungalows is likely to feel uncomfortable after a while.) It is not a bad idea to look at an Ordnance Survey Map to see if there are any airfields or sewage works close by,

NO WINDOWS'

IF THE OWNER ASKS WHY
YOU DO NOT LIKE THE
PROPERTY - TELL HIM WHY
    POLITELY .

Ebbage.

especially if you are looking in the country. Visit the
locality at different times of the day or evening, e.g. rush
hours or school leaving times. Do not wait until it is too
late.

If you feel that this could be the property for you, look
at your motives and requirements again. Are you making
any compromises? If so, think about the consequences
not only now, but at all times of the year and in varying
circumstances into the future. Although you will not feel
much like it, try and look on the bleak side to try and get
matters into the correct perspective. Still want it? Then
now is the time to check that your furniture will fit, so

measure anything doubtful ready for your second visit and make your appointment, sooner rather than later. You will kick yourself if you leave it for a few days and the property is under offer.

Preparing To Offer

On this visit although you are going to be verifying the suitability of the property, you should also begin to adopt your negotiating stance. What is included? It is usually safe to assume that everything mentioned on the particulars is included, but let the owner show you from room to room telling you what he intends to leave and make a note of everything. Additionally, make a note of everything that is screwed to the wall and going – the resulting holes may mean the room needs redecorating. Along the same lines, with the owner's permission lift a picture from the wall, especially one above a radiator; there is bound to be a mark and you will have made your point. Try and open each window – say nothing as the owner explains that they always stick when the wind is in the west, but make a note. Are carpets and curtains included in the price? Whether the answer is yes or no make a note of those you want; if they are included and you only want the bedroom carpets you can use this to justify a reduction and if they are not you can make your offer subject to their inclusion. In the garden, especially if it is newly planted, make a point of asking if they are leaving all the plants. It is not practical to list them but make a point of being seen to note what is there. This may seem extreme but often an expensive shrub or two will disappear and in one case a vendor took the lawn of his small garden with him!

Ask the owner about his own situation. Has he found a property? If so, is he being pressed? He will be a lot keener to find a buyer for his own property if this is the

AT ALL TIMES KEEP YOUR RELATIONS
AS CORDIAL AS POSSIBLE.

case. At all times keep relations as cordial as possible.

Once you are away from the property, consider the highest price you are willing to pay and a suitable starting point for negotiations. The former is going to be dictated by a personal view as a property is worth different prices to different people, but make sure that you can justify even your starting point by reference to comparable properties you have seen.

Negotiating
If your vendor is using an agent, you should negotiate through him, but it does not do any harm to ask the same questions of both parties to make sure that the answers do not differ. However, some vendors passionately

dislike direct discussion over prices and feel strongly that this is the agent's job; if they make this clear, stick to their wishes or you will only annoy them and probably lose out to someone who respects their viewpoint. A good agent at this time should be able to give you the impression that he is really on your side whilst still remaining loyal to his client. When you have prepared your offer, including all you want within that figure, it is sufficient to submit it verbally, but back it up with a letter confirming the call. At all times make such communications subject to contract.

It is a good idea to ask the agent a few questions before letting your offer be known. What does he think the vendor will take? Most agents will reply the asking price, but it is worth a try. Have there been any offers yet? You may be told a figure that has been rejected and will almost certainly be told if somebody else is interested. This is important, as a favoured lever to encourage higher offers is the introduction of a rival bidder. If you are told that there is another party involved, try and verify it, subtly, by speaking to the vendor, who might even tell you if your rival is in a better or worse position if handled carefully.

Remember to stress the advantages of your position when submitting your offer, especially if you have found a buyer. If you haven't, emphasise the good viewing rate. The agent will ask if he can help with your property if it is in his area, probably pointing out that it will make life simpler if both sales are handled from the same office. This is quite a large source of new instructions for many agents as applicants often feel they have a better chance of getting their offer accepted if they sell through the agent acting for their proposed purchase. It should make no difference, so if you feel you are being pressured in this direction make the hint that the matter is not being wholly dealt with in the vendor's interest and make a mental note to be wary of anything this agent says. It is a fact, however, that an agent will pay more interest to a sale in the contract stage if two fees depend on it. Whether this is sufficient reason for him to handle both, bearing in mind the potential conflicts of interest is debatable.

The same principle applies to mortgages – if you are given the impression that your offer stands a better chance if you arrange your mortgage through the vendor's agent, protest at once. Having said that, if the mortgage the agent can offer is as good as the best from another source it makes sense to arrange it through him, as you will be giving him additional financial incentive with no potential conflict of interest acting against you.

There is no set rule about it, but more often than not, an agent will recommend rejection of first offers on principle. You must judge by the personalities involved, but if you are starting low, do not make it a silly offer; this does nothing for your credibility and only irritates the vendor and agent. If you have stored up a formidable list of points to justify your low offer, do not reveal all at once. Mention a comparable property or two that show your offer in a good light. Do not list all the property's faults, 'there is an awful lot of work to do' is enough at first. The comment will be relayed to the vendor who, having been present when you quietly made your observations, will know what you mean, and may even think that you have noticed things that you haven't. Confidence is crucial. Under no circumstances admit to any flexibility in your offer, but do not say that it is final when it is not – retain your integrity.

If your offer is rejected, listen carefully to the reasons and let them sweat a little while you consider the matter.

Counter comparables will probably be cited and it is at this point that another interested party might appear. One reason for rejection frequently heard is that the vendor has got to get x thousand pounds more or he cannot move. Take this one with a pinch of salt and point out that this factor has absolutely no bearing on the value of the property.

When you go back remind them of your comparables and bring out the detail justifying work necessary to bring the property up to standard. You should still be looking at other properties; point this out. If you are in a good position, having sold to a cash buyer or similar, stress this again and again as a good offer is worth nothing without the ability to complete. You will have had to raise your offer unless you have found additional reasons for the price reduction you seek or are pretty sure no other bidders are about. Do not fall into the trap of thinking of every £1000 increase as only another few pounds on the mortgage. Think in terms of bundles of ten pound notes and you will be more careful.

The process continues until there is an agreement or an uncrossable gulf. Should you get very near and still get stuck, reconsider all the extras, maybe a concession on some of those will show enough goodwill to bridge the gap. Pride is often as important as financial necessity in negotiation.

In most market conditions these basics should serve you well. If the market is quiet you can afford to spin the whole business out over a long period, but beware of annoying the vendor and creating an atmosphere of ill-will. When the market is moving at a frantic pace and purchasers are being gazumped, if the asking price is right, go straight to it and in order to safeguard your position once your offer is accepted, try and build up a personal relationship with the vendor. At the same time keep a careful check that the property is not still being offered and do not let your solicitor lose a day through complacency.

Sometimes sealed bids are invited for a property, usually when it is in need of work and/or being sold by executors. (Properties in need of work are dealt with in a separate section.) This usually involves inviting offers that will not be negotiable, by a specific time. Having seen so many people torturing themselves over such situations, I am sure that the best advice one can give is to offer the highest price you are prepared to pay, to the extent that if it goes for any more, you wouldn't have wanted it. If your bid is successful, do not ask by how much as you will gain nothing but regret and self-recrimination. You got what you wanted at a price you were prepared to pay.

In conclusion, these guidelines will help you to deal with many situations but always take careful stock of the personalities involved, your own included. If it is contrary to your nature to negotiate, do not try; you have to be confident – similarly if you get the impression that the vendor will have a very short fuse, tread carefully. The majority of people appreciate that negotiation is accepted practice within property dealings, however, so keep your wits about you and you should do well.

The Contract Stage
The contract stage has been dealt with under 'Estate Agents' Procedure' (page 62) and 'Selling your Property Without An Estate Agent', (page 96) but there are a few relevant aspects worth mentioning from the buyer's angle.

Once your offer is accepted, you will be under close scrutiny for any signs of reticence, by the vendor and his agent (if he is doing his job properly). Demonstrate your keenness by immediately instructing your solicitor to proceed, arranging a surveyor and applying for a mortgage. When confirming your offer to your solicitor do not forget to list any extras included in the price, together with your estimate of their value as they will not be liable for Stamp Duty. Your solicitor will confirm the apportionment with the vendor's solicitor.

You may be asked for a preliminary deposit by an agent, as distinct from the 10% deposit required by the vendor's solicitor just prior to exchange of contracts. Many agents have stopped taking deposits over the past few years, as laws to safeguard the public make systems increasingly cumbersome. Rarely do feelings get so heated over such a trivial matter. The reluctant applicant points out that he will be losing interest, although with deposits rarely exceeding £200 this is not significant and the piqued agent will express doubt as to the applicant's keenness to proceed, even though a deposit has to be returnable at any time. Conversely, some applicants are very keen to put pen to cheque book in order to give themselves a sense of security and many agents do not welcome the administrative costs of taking deposits. If you are asked for one and feel inclined to pay, ensure that the receipt states that it is returnable upon request and is headed Subject to Contract. It is often not worthwhile jeopardising goodwill for the sake of a few pounds in interest.

If you have had your offer accepted in a very active market where gazumping is a worry, keep in close touch with the agent and vendor all the way, never letting the latter forget his personal commitment. Ask for a draft contract immediately and for the property to be taken off the market. Under any circumstances, as long as all parties keep each other up-to-date with new developments throughout the contract stage nobody should have reason to complain. Unfortunately communication is not always what it should be so it is important that you keep your end up by keeping the vendor or his agent well informed of your situation and, if applicable, that of the chain behind you. Having said that, use your judgment of the individual again, and refrain from regaling him nightly with tales of your buyer's buyer's buyer if it obviously bores him to tears.

Ensure your solicitor is quickly in receipt of a draft contract and get him to ask why if he is not. The vendor may be playing games or his solicitor may just be awaiting receipt of the deeds from a building society or bank. If you have a tricky vendor who tries to run a contract race, his solicitor is obliged under Law Society Rules to notify your solicitor.

Surveys often cause rifts between purchasers and vendors, mostly through misunderstandings. Even though you are paying for it, the building society/bank survey is being carried out on their behalf not yours, primarily to ensure that their loan is adequately secured. Prior to 1980 the proposed purchaser had no right of access to the report, but an important test case altered that situation so that now the purchaser does have some redress for negligence. Such surveys usually lack detail and often the valuation is on the cautious side. Do not worry too much about this; as long as it secures the loan, the building society or bank will be happy. It is a mistake to try and re-open negotiations if it is a few thousand adrift from the price you are paying (especially if the market is leaping ahead); surveyors are understandably cautious by nature.

When you receive your Full Structural Survey, or House Buyers Report, do remember that you have requested a list of the property's faults so it is unlikely to make cheerful reading. Every property has its faults but what you are looking for are the serious ones. If your report does reveal a serious problem that you had not anticipated when making your offer, the first thing to do is decide whether you want to take on the repairs if an adjustment is made to the price. If you do, then get quotes for the work as quickly as possible and present

your case in a fair manner. Most people are reasonable under such circumstances and will compromise but inevitably there are those who are sufficiently confident of their position to say take it or leave it. In a very active market, prices may have moved up sufficiently to cover the extra expenditure in theory and the vendor will not hesitate to point this out, but remember that he has probably got a vendor pressing him to proceed quickly and starting with a new purchaser will cause him a delay.

So, answer letters promptly and keep a close eye on the proceedings and you should be ready to exchange contracts without unnecessary delay or problems. Your solicitor will request a 10% deposit ready to be transferred to the vendor's solicitor upon exchange of contracts and the usual practice is for the purchaser of your property to give permission for you to use his 10% deposit and then you make up any difference. This will be held in a special client's account that is covered by an indemnity scheme, so you need not worry in the unlikely event of your solicitor taking a prolonged holiday in Rio de Janiero.

Once exchange of contracts has taken place your moving arrangements can be confirmed and your solicitor should deal with the detailed mortgage arrangements etc., but something often overlooked is that it is important to insure the property you have contracted to purchase because if it is burned down at this point, the contract still stands. Mortgage lenders normally include this in their arrangements with you, handling the insurance on your behalf and incorporating the cost into your repayments; however, this is not always the case, so make sure what is happening. It's your liability.

This is also the time to make sure all the services, i.e. gas, electricity, telephone are transferred to you. A

"IN THE UNLIKELY EVENT OF YOUR
SOLICITOR TAKING A PROLONGED
HOLIDAY".

surprising number of people forget and spend a few days incommunicado as a result. Your solicitor may deal with the apportionment of general and water rates, but you must remember to notify everybody from the DVLC to your grandmother of your new address.

Oh, and don't forget to cancel the papers and milk.

Private Sales

In chasing private advertisements and sale boards you are going to come across very different attitudes ranging from the people who think that all you have to do to sell a house is paint 'For Sale' on a piece of hardboard to those who will deal with the matter with great efficiency, possibly better than some of the agents you will have encountered. They have one thing in common, the desire to save estate agents' fees. This could be to your advantage and mean a saving for you too, although if the vendor has read the relevant section in this book he will argue, quite correctly, that since he is taking on the work and expenses of an estate agent, *he* should benefit from the fact that he will not have to pay any fees.

The main danger when buying privately is the fellow who does not realise what he is taking on. You will spot him quite early as he is unlikely to have prepared any particulars, will not know what he is leaving in the way of fixtures and fittings and will take very little interest in your situation. You must be careful not to frighten him off during the negotiation stage, especially if you (having read this book) obviously know a lot more about buying and selling property than he does. His confidence is likely to be brittle, especially after he has accepted an offer when major doubts of his own ability will be surfacing. The chances are that the more lively of the local agents will be worrying him with claims that they can get him a higher price, even after paying their fees. This might be true if he has not researched his asking price properly. He might do any number of strange things, such as keeping his property on the market after he has agreed to sell, or even putting it with an agent. If you come across somebody like this, be firm with him and let him know that you will withdraw at once unless he takes the property off the market otherwise you will stand to lose money spent on surveyors and solicitors. If he does give you a clear run, remember that he has not got an agent to advise him of the usual practices so watch him very carefully – he might be one of those who thinks it is smart to wait until you are nearly ready to exchange before proceeding on his own purchase. It can be difficult to make him see reason over serious unforeseen problems revealed in your survey, so give yourself every chance by meeting him at the property and explaining the trouble carefully. You must be a patient person to deal with the unprepared private vendor.

The fellow who knows what he is doing is a different matter altogether. No kid gloves should be necessary when dealing with him so you can adopt a straightforward attitude. He will prefer it that way. He might be a harder negotiator but at least you will know where you are with him.

More often than not, a private purchase is quite satisfactory and gives both parties a pleasing feeling of having beaten the system.

Property in Need of Renovation

Many people like the idea of renovating an old property but only a few have the drive to go through with it. If you are thinking along these lines, examine your motives: it can be the best way of getting a property the way you want it, you might have building skills or be a D.I.Y. enthusiast, it might be all you can afford or you may just have a romantic notion of the idea. Of these reasons, the last two are the most perilous; it is a serious mistake to be underfinanced when taking on a renovation and even though the end product may be wonderful, there is nothing romantic about the worry, hard work and discomfort that is involved.

It is a good idea to talk to friends who have done it, if possible. Ignore their beautiful home and let them tell you about the upheaval; living for weeks without carpets amongst dust and piles of rubble, the cold if the heating was not installed in time, bathing at friends' houses whilst they had no facilities, the constant smell of paint, the troubles with builders, electricians, plumbers and Local Authorities. The lack of free time.

If you are still keen then start giving yourself an idea of

the cost of the work you will have to have done by a professional. Roofing, plumbing, wiring, damp-proofing, timber treatment and heating installation are beyond most mortals, so get an idea of their costs to make sure you are not wasting your time. Obtain details of Local Authority Grants and their availability in your area – these are usually only for properties in the lower price range but if you are renovating a listed building, whatever the value, you may qualify for an Historic Buildings Grant. Attitudes and resources vary so much from one Local Authority to another that it is difficult to generalise but in all cases their procedure must be followed to the letter. Some Authorities can be remarkably swift and helpful whilst others spin the affair out for so long that it might not be worth the wait. In some instances the time of year can make a difference to availability, as that year's allocation may have been used up.

Your building society/bank should be consulted – make sure it is not one that looks unfavourably on the type of property you seek – if they do seem reluctant, there are plenty who will want to help so shop around. You will almost certainly be told that a retention will be made. This means that a proportion of the mortgage money will be held back until various essential works are carried out to the required standard. It will be necessary to take out a short-term bank loan to cover the period while the work is being carried out so speak to your bank manager.

Which brings you to the property. It is likely that the sight of a cheap house in need of work advertised in the local paper will have contributed to your wanting to take this course in the first place. This will have given you only a very vague idea of prices as you do not know the work that will be needed to bring it up to standard. Each property must be taken as a separate case and your touchstone should be what the property is worth when it is finished. For estate agents, valuing such property is a headache; in theory they should be able to arrive at a value by subtracting the cost of renovation from the value of the property in good order, taking into account Local Authority grants if applicable. In practice the lowest price obtained is likely to be from a property dealer renovating for profit, taking into account not only the renovation costs but also the cost of his overdraft and a profit to make the project worthwhile. As grants are only available to individual owner occupiers they will not apply either. This situation tends to arise mostly when the property is in such a bad state it even puts off the enthusiasts. Dry rot is frequently a cause of such dilapidation. At the other extreme is the builder who wants the property for his own occupation. He might qualify for a grant and will only have to take into account the cost of materials. Add to this a scarcity value and it will help to understand the extraordinary prices sometimes paid for property in need of work. As a result of this anomaly, prices given on sales particulars are only a rough guide rounded to the nearest five or ten thousand pounds.

Properties in need of renovation are most frequently offered through estate agents and many of these will be executors' sales where the best prices must be seen to have been obtained. As a result they will be advertised for a week or two before a buyer is settled upon, but keep in touch with the agents nevertheless, as sometimes a property will flash on and off the market unadvertised, and you want to make sure that you get a look in. You will get to know the agents most likely to be instructed to deal with the type of property you seek – only a few will have the necessary close relationship with local solicitors that results in instructions on an executors' sale. Constant contact with these agents confirms your seriousness and will give you an opportunity to show that you know what you are talking about. This is important as nothing attracts dreamers and timewasters like property in need of work and it can be of great assistance if the agent has confidence in your knowledge.

So the property is on the market – you and hoards of sightseers and a few other serious applicants have looked over and on first inspection it looks as if it might be a viable proposition – where to from here? First of all find out how much time you have got, ask the agent whether he has set a date for final offers or can give you a vague idea when this will be. Most will oblige. Next get your builders/electricians/plumbers around. Ask for estimates verbally as soon as possible to be followed up in writing. If you are obtaining more than one set of estimates be certain that they are all pricing the same work. It is easier to get one builder to oversee the work you cannot do as he will be experienced in co-ordination. This will be more expensive than running the job yourself but it does take a lot of the pressure off you and mistakes do not come cheap at this point. Although one reason you may be taking on such a project is to get a house just the way you want it, have an eye for the resale potential – a jacuzzi in the living room may be your idea of luxury, but this view is not universal. You may want to take into financial consideration the work that you will have to do, but the degree of consideration you give it is up to you – be warned, a lot of people do not think about it. If you are hoping to obtain a Local Authority grant check that the property qualifies. You would be well advised not to make your offer conditional upon the grant, as agents will be more aware than you of the delays this can cause, but it might be worth a try so sound out the agent.

Once the figures are in you will be able to work out your offer. Bear in mind the value of the completed project. Put aside a contingency sum as there is bound to be trouble you are not expecting. On the other hand, do remember that if you are particular about decor, you are likely to want to redecorate any property you buy, whatever the condition. If there is a lot of interest, which is usual, the agent is likely to invite final offers so go to the highest figure you will want to pay at once. Remember – if it goes higher you wouldn't have wanted it. When confirming your offer in writing (Subject to Contract of course) verify that you have taken into account the need for rewiring, damp-proofing, reroofing or whatever the necessary works might be. Add to this details of your own sale if applicable – another instance when it is important to have a good buyer. You will thus reassure the agent and help your case. If the interest is thin, then putting forward a case for an offer lower than you are prepared to go is not going to be difficult, but be sure of your ground when doing this.

The agent is sometimes put into an awkward situation once the offers are in, as quite often the highest figure will come from someone who obviously doesn't know what he is taking on and is likely to waste everybody's time and money by withdrawing after a few weeks. This is why it is so important to have given him confidence in your keenness, knowledge and competence. The agent will confer with his client and put forward not only the figures but also his opinion of the reliability of the offer.

If somebody offers over you, have no regrets; you should have done all that was possible and could not have done better. The experience will have been valuable and should sharpen you for next time. Make a note to enquire, about once a week, about the progress of the successful applicant – not with gazumping in mind but in case he gets second thoughts. That way you are likely to be the first notified if he withdraws and you can jump straight in. (This course is often desirable for agents as it saves readvertising, recirculation of details and most irritating, showing scores of people around again.)

Should you be successful with your offer, apply for your grant and waste no time in getting a Full Structural Survey carried out. If you and your builder have kept your eyes open this should not reveal anything too horrific, but if for example, dry rot is uncovered that you have not taken into your calculations, you will be justified in trying to renegotiate. Expect resistance but point out that you had not taken it into account as shown in your written offer and that it is extremely unlikely that anybody else who offered did either.

As with any purchase, get your solicitor and building society/bank into action as quickly as possible to allow time to iron out any problems. You will want to get the building work carried out as fast as possible so, as long as it fits in with the builder's availability, try and get permission to have access to the property and start work between exchange and completion. This can be done by giving an undertaking to finish any work started in the unlikely event of you failing to complete. Solicitors vary in their attitudes on works before completion, but it is worth a try as it may enable you to get some messy work out of the way before you move in – such as knocking down a wall and removing the rubble.

From here on the purchase should proceed as any other, so keep pushing for exchange – you are not safe until then. The rest is up to you. There is a lot of hard work ahead but it will be worth it in the end.

As a final note, should you get in financial trouble half-way through a renovation, do everything possible to avoid selling the property part-finished as this is one way of losing a great deal of money. Beg or borrow the money to finish or do a deal with a builder – do anything you can to make sure you get the benefit of the potential you saw at the beginning.

The Purchase of New Property
Like the idea of renovating an old cottage, to some people this is a dream come true, to others a ghastly prospect. One factor that is impossible to ignore is that this is probably the easiest and quickest way to buy property.

For a start, you move into a newly fitted, newly decorated property. If the builder has done his job properly there should be no unpleasant surprises such as the goo that has been accumulating behind the previous owner's cooker for years or that the carpet under his sofa has a huge red wine stain on it. The property should have an N.H.B.C. (National House Builders Council) guarantee, otherwise you may have troubles with your mortgage. This is a ten year guarantee, the first two years of which are the builder's liability, giving a general cover. If you have made a complaint in writing during this period and the builder doesn't respond or has gone bankrupt then the matter should be referred to the N.H.B.C. Outside this period the cover is purely for structural and load bearing problems and should be referred direct to the N.H.B.C.

Another factor that facilitates the purchase of a new property is that there is no dependent chain of sales beyond. In addition to this, any agent acting on the sale of a new property, and this is very often an employee of the builder these days, will be instructed to keep a very close eye on your sale and the associated chain. The principal reason for this is that builders work on enormous overdrafts with correspondingly large interest payments and the longer it takes to sell, the less profit he will make. As a result of efficient scrutiny of the chain in the contract stage, delays are spotted early and avoided and sales are speeded up which benefits all parties.

Of course there are many other reasons why one should want to buy a new property apart from the speed of the transaction. From the aesthetic point of view you will dictate the internal appearance from scratch and avoid paying for other people's taste in decor that you intend to dispose of. On the same line, the general appearance of new residential property is given a great deal more consideration these days by architects and builders. On the exterior more roof slopes, dormers, gables, dentils etc., together with rendering, cosmetic timbering and sympathetic choice of brick types give today's new properties more character and take them a long way from the 'little boxes' of the sixties and seventies. On estates it is less usual to see lines of houses exactly the same. House types are mixed and plots angled to avoid that ghastly uniform effect. More interest is given to the interior with fireplaces, cornices, fitted kitchens and bedrooms and tiled bathrooms. Turfing of gardens tends to be standard practice these days too.

Low maintenance and running costs are another strong point. Many new properties have minimum maintenance exterior woodwork and are sold with loft and cavity wall insulation, double glazing and full central heating.

There are many sales incentives too – some for early exchange of contracts, some all in. Although the value of these is debatable as it is often maintained that one pays for them within the asking price, they should not be ignored. Free conveyancing, low cost mortgages, fitted carpets, holidays, cars – look at each, calculating its value to you.

With all the aforementioned advantages, why do people ever buy anything other than a new property? Inevitably there is a price to pay. The figures quoted in the sales brochure are very rarely negotiable and may seem a little high when comparing the accommodation with similar older properties and the builder's selling agent is not looking so closely at the chain relating to your sale for your benefit alone. If there is a break, somebody drops out or a mortgage is refused, then the builder will look at the new position from a commercial, not a compassionate point of view. In this event you are likely to be given quite a short period of time to find a completed chain or the property will be re-marketed, possibly at a higher price.

Always remember that although the builder has his standards and good name to maintain, he is in business for profit and adjusts his attitudes and practices accordingly. One manifestation of this may well be in the form of a non-returnable deposit requested to reserve the property you want. Should the transaction go ahead as planned, it should be deducted from the final payments but if it does not, whether it is your fault or not, you will forfeit the money. This practice is by no means universal but always look carefully at any conditions relating to deposits when purchasing new property.

Another disadvantage is that new houses tend to be smaller and are situated on smaller plots than older properties. Once more this is a commercial consideration since obviously the greater number of properties to the acre and the lower the building costs, the higher the profit. The problem of smaller kitchens and bedrooms is sometimes negated by ingenious use of the available space when planning the location of fitted units and furniture. A smaller plot is likely to result in less privacy, but you may consider it an advantage as there will be less garden to maintain.

Maintenance of a small new garden may be easy, but stocking it is not. Bringing a garden up to standard from a newly turfed building plot requires considerable effort and expenditure. New trees, shrubs and plants do not come cheap and the soil is likely to be poor and need building up. The garden, indeed the whole area if it is a large scale development, will take some years to mature and gain any appeal.

Inside the property there are likely to be teething problems, for example plaster shrinkage, which will be made good by most builders but is a nuisance.

When looking at new property it is important to ascertain the extent to which the builder is going to finish the property. It will probably just be painted throughout but check; he may be prepared to put up wallpaper. Tiling in the bathroom could mean one line of tiles around the bath or a complete job. Will you have a choice of bathroom suite? Ask precisely what is included in the way of kitchen units and if you exchange early enough, will you be able to have some say in the layout? Will curtain rails be put up? What about shelves? Try to think of all those fittings you take for granted in your old property because they were there when you moved in. As with all extras, list them in the letter confirming your offer to purchase (Subject to Contract) to avoid misunderstandings.

The earlier you exchange contracts on a new property, the more control you are going to have over the fixtures, fittings and finish. It is understandable that a builder is not going to be very enthusiastic about painting a house dark green, if that is your wish, if he is not 100% certain you are buying it.

Once you have exchanged, make sure the builder keeps to your timetable; the pressure is considerably lessened for him once he has a contract and he may be tempted to use his labour on more urgent matters. Apart from the usual applications for services, make sure you apply for a telephone at once, as this can be seriously delayed as it is a new installation.

Finally, on the day you move, make sure your new property is easily found by the removal men. The road names and house numbers may not be up, so clear instructions are essential if you do not want your belongings doing a tour of the area.

Purchasing Property at Auction

The most important point to realise when considering purchase by auction is that if you are successful in your bid, you will be required to exchange contracts and give a deposit there and then. This means that establishment of title, Local Authority Searches, arrangement of mortgage and survey will all have to be dealt with before you know whether you can purchase the property. Obviously this means that you run the risk of spending money to no avail, but you also stand a far better chance of buying a genuine bargain at auction.

The most common lots at residential property auctions are tenanted and part tenanted properties. The former will not interest you as an owner occupier, being purchased for investment purposes only, but the latter can be of interest to those who enjoy speculation and have patience. The tenants will be protected, so you will be obliged to wait until they vacate voluntarily, but in the meantime you will have your own accommodation and will certainly make a handsome profit when you do gain full possession. The main drawback in taking this course is that building societies do not look favourably upon part tenanted properties, so you will probably need to be a cash buyer.

Vacant dilapidated properties being sold at auction are likely to be of most interest to the owner occupier. It is not difficult to see why a vendor might choose to sell in this manner if you bear in mind the time that can be wasted in trying to sell such properties conventionally. Instant commitment to purchase has a lot to be said for it if you want to use the money for another project or even just bank it. The main disadvantage for the vendor is that auctions mostly attract dealers who will want to make a profit and prices are correspondingly low. This, of course, is to the advantage of the potential owner occupier.

If a potential bargain attracts you, get an idea from the auctioneer of the price range he expects it to fall into, get your builders around and work out your figures, not forgetting that you will probably have to service a hefty bridging loan while you sell your own property. If it looks good and you are able to finance it, try an offer before auction: not your best offer, but something a bit higher than the auctioneer has anticipated. He is obliged to submit the offer to his client and even if he does not accept it, he may tell you what he will take. If it is obvious that the vendor wants to see what his property will fetch under the hammer then get your solicitor and surveyor into action and be prepared for the big day.

At the auction, do not be afraid of scratching your ear at the wrong time in case you buy something you do not want. The auctioneer knows very quickly who the serious bidders are and will be careful to push each lot to its limit. Do not get carried away. Fix your limit and stick to it. No regrets if it goes over – either try again or stick to more conventional methods.

The only other types of property sold at auction that are likely to be of interest to the private buyer are those which are so bizarre that putting a price on them is nearly impossible. For example, a house in three acres of

PROPERTIES SOLD IN THIS MANNER WILL TEND TO BE OUT OF THE ORDINARY

ground, part of which is a scrap yard or a disused water tower. If one of these catches your eye, think hard and long about it because if it is difficult to sell once, the chances are it will be again.

Bargain property can be bought at auction and although more owner occupiers are buying this way, it is still for the few as private bridging finance is difficult to arrange.

7

ESTATE AGENTS: ANGELS OR DEVILS? WHERE CAN THEY GO FROM HERE?

This book would not be complete without a few more observations on the lot of the estate agent.

If your sister or daughter announces that she is dating an estate agent, the immediate image that comes to mind might be of a rather sharp, overbearing man with a second-hand Porsche. You may be right, quite a few do drive second-hand Porsches, but the chances are that you would be surprised when you met him and found yourself saying that he is not a typical estate agent. Not many do fit into the category defined by the public's image but that image refuses to go away, as does the general bad reputation of agents in their business dealings. As you will have realised from the contents of this book, I am under no illusions as to the various trickeries, temptations and short-comings of the business but I am also aware that many of them are as a result of a wasteful, flawed system, the evolution of which is as much the fault of the public as it is of the agents.

Almost everybody has their favourite estate agent horror story. In anticipation of writing this I have been asking friends and acquaintances for theirs over the last few weeks and it was interesting to note how many of them actually were as a result of bad business and how many were not the estate agent's fault at all. It was about fifty fifty, but the estate agents got the blame for the lot. Most of the problems not caused by agents were actually attributable to unscrupulous vendors and the remainder to solicitors but if in doubt, people blame the agent. Why is this?

Estate agents are unpopular and the public is suspicious of them. This starts matters off on the wrong foot straightaway – any relationship formed on such a basis is fighting against the odds and bound to make both parties defensive. People buying and selling property are often very tense – they are dealing with sums of money and situations that are normally outside their experience and it can have some bizarre effects. Some start behaving in a manner they associate with property tycoons, I suppose associating aggression with high finance. Others, whom one must assume are only averagely avaricious under normal circumstances, make Shylock seem like Father Christmas, as their greed is magnified by the size of the transaction. Then there is the 'Arthur Daly type' who becomes positively serpentine when asked to make any serious commitment. Worst of all though, is the nouveau-ruthless 'J.R. Ewing type' who starts renegotiating the day before exchange of contracts and if you do go ahead with him, will probably complete three days later on principle. All probably wonderful people who love their mothers, but sit one in front of an estate agent and his face and hands become hairy, his forehead bulges and he grows fangs. Of course many people behave in a reasonable manner, but it is fair to say that the estate agent does not always see the public at its best.

The difficult nature of estate agent/vendor and estate agent/applicant relationships is a cause of many difficulties. Both are supposed to be clearly defined but this does not always appear to be the case to the public.

The agent receives his instructions from the vendor and markets the property, presenting it in the best possible light. If it is located next to a two hundred foot high factory chimney his photograph omits this, as does his description. This is quite reasonable looking at it from the vendor's point of view, but the applicant who has to make a hundred mile round trip to see the property is unlikely to see it that way. Often such an applicant will drive straight on without even knocking on the door, cursing estate agents one and all, leaving an irate vendor waiting around for yet another apparently non-existent applicant, also thinking dark thoughts about agents. Let that agent suggest mentioning the problem on the particulars though, and he will find himself minus one instruction. Although the agent is instructed by the vendor he clearly has obligations to the applicant too. Every estate agent has experienced applicants sifting through sheaves of details in front of him making adverse comments on the area, construction, size or condition of his various clients' properties – he has to agree with some of the observations in spite of the confict with his loyalty to his client. Vendors would scream blue murder if they heard how their properties were sometimes discussed, but it is necessary for the agent to be frank with applicants in order to retain his credibility that is so important during negotiations.

When battle commences the agent treads a fine line, for he genuinely wants the applicant to succeed in his aims and do a deal, but he has to ensure that his client obtains, and knows he has obtained, the best possible price. When he goes back to the applicant the news that his offer has been rejected will be softened with sympathy and an explanation of the factors that make it reasonable to pay more. The disappointed and irritated applicant's attitude is often one of "You would say that, wouldn't you?" but gradually he will lose his first flush of ire and may come back with another offer – not what the vendor asked for, but an increase. Upon submitting this, with all the relevant reasons for acceptance, the disappointed and irritated vendor's attitude is often one of "All you are worried about is your commission". The agent might lose and regain the trust of both parties several times during a negotiation. On many occasions a vendor is left with the feeling that his agent has been acting against him because of the necessity to argue the applicant's case. If the agent was saying anything to do a deal he might be correct to make this charge, but often the agent is just pointing out that an applicant has offered a fair price and is justifying the statement.

The emotional factor that is bound to be present when selling residential property creates problems unlike any other business. As an example of this, in the latter days of my career in estate agency I was involved in trying to sell a piece of land suitable for one house to a partner of one of the large commercial and industrial estate agents in London. This fellow wanted the land badly, as it was the only way he was going to be able to get the house he wanted and single plots were scarce. My client, who didn't really need the money, was very fond of the part of his garden that constituted the plot and was a wily old chap, who had been in business all his life. Needless to say, the estate agent was no sluggard when it came to negotiation. The negotiation was protracted to say the least – it would take at least five thousand words to describe it in full, but suffice to say that it culminated in a ten day squabble over a crop of apples and the replacement of a garden shed. The agent got his land in the end, but the poor fellow was tearing his hair out over the closing stages. A man who was used to negotiating for properties worth millions of pounds was nearly driven to distraction, mainly because he was dealing with a vendor's whims as opposed to his calculations and comparables. He vowed that he would not touch residential agency with a twenty foot barge pole.

Gazumping is invariably blamed on estate agents but as usual, the situation is not black and white. The circumstance when an agent is to blame is usually when the property is on the market with more than one firm. Agent A receives an offer, the vendor accepts it and instructs Agents B and C to stop offering, much to their annoyance. Agent B, being the sort of person that estate agency can well do without, might 'forget' to take the property out of his advert, or more subtly, might just keep it in mind for the right applicant. This applicant appears, money burning a hole in his pocket, and, unable to offer him anything else, the agent shows him details of the property that is under offer. It is just what the applicant is looking for so it is conspiratorial winks all round and "I'll get you an appointment". The vendor resists at first but the agent is very persuasive, probably pointing out that it will do him no harm to have such a good prospect as first reserve. If the applicant wants the property he is obliged to offer a higher price than that already agreed which the vendor turns down at first, but when the increase is too much for him to turn down, he accepts. He tells Agent A, who has the unenviable task of informing the original proposed purchaser and, if he does not want to lose his commission, trying to persuade him to better the new offer. Naturally the original proposed purchaser is less than delighted and looks for the nearest scapegoat – Agent A. If he really wants the property and is prepared to swallow his pride negotiations carry on, back and forth, until finances call a halt to one party but however it ends, both agents emerge with tarnished reputations even though it is only

Agent B who has behaved so disgracefully.

Agents can also be responsible for a gazump through inefficiency by not checking out all interested parties before his vendor accepts an offer. This is just bad business practice and although this fellow deserves all the abuse that is coming to him, at least he hasn't been consciously immoral.

Many gazumps are unforeseeable however, and all good agents dread them. The applicant comes out of the blue, perhaps having seen the property three weeks earlier and abused it without mercy when asked for an opinion. If he comes in with a better offer after a sale has been agreed, the agent has no option but to submit it. There is no argument about this. The agent's reputation is thus at the mercy of his client's moral standards and there is nothing he can do about it. Estate agents are very vulnerable in this situation.

Gazumping is a problem that has got to be overcome – insurance policies will only mask the symptoms, not provide a cure. Only legislation or a radical change in the system can do that. It is only the loose morals of vendors that can cause it, but in nine cases out of ten the agent is blamed – often when he is not at fault. For this reason it is very much in the interests of estate agents to do something about it. So why don't they?

Lack of cohesion and not wanting to derail the gravy train are probably the main reasons. Most agents would agree that the system needs change to one degree or another, but you would be hard pushed to get them to agree on the nature of the problems, let alone the answer to them.

Of course gazumping is only one aspect of the flawed system which receives a good deal of publicity. It goes much deeper. A system where the successes finance such a high degree of failure is wrong – it is just not fair on those who do sell. A system where the vendor is not liable for the amount spent in trying to sell his property is wrong – he would adopt a different attitude if it were otherwise. A system that allows such a long period between agreement in principle and legal commitment is wrong – this enables both vendors and proposed purchasers to change their minds without liability. The high level of waste and the consequent high level of fees is tolerated by the public for the sake of the No Sale, No Fee principle and to a lesser extent the option to instruct more than one agent at a time. The public, in trying to save money just in case their properties do not sell, end up spending a great deal more than necessary. Both sides are to blame for the current situation, leading each other on into a mire of inefficiency, but whereas some agents might be reluctant to change anything that might jeopardise their fee income, the public, I believe, would welcome change enthusiastically as long as it had confidence in the new system. It is a wonderful thought that a more efficient system will evolve in time. Sometimes evolution needs a nudge.

Any new system is going to need to be based on a higher degree of trust and unfortunately it is an unavoidable fact that estate agency currently attracts an undesirable element, lacking scruples or any desire to improve their service if it doesn't increase their income. I believe the advent of the huge chains of agents built up by the financial service giants from the City offers an excellent opportunity for the business to raise its standards and polish its tarnished reputation. By building up public confidence through the elimination of sharp practice and good training programmes they should find themselves in a position where they can change the system over such a wide field that the independents will be forced to follow.

The most logical step is to offer a service based on the amount of work done for a client. It would have to be very carefully worked at to maintain an incentive to make a sale go through, probably by having a bonus payable upon completion, but with sufficient financial backing I am sure the public would flock to the innovator. Perhaps the Boards of these companies will not want to risk derailing the gravy train by changing the nature of the businesses they have acquired to such a radical extent, but once they have settled in, it will undoubtedly be within their power.

Even gazumping could be reduced enormously by a degree of co-operation within the property business. Imagine all vendors being required to have a Local Authority Search and a survey in hand before they can market their property. Also, all applicants being required to get their mortgage references taken up before making an offer. Then, once their solicitors verify that the title is not faulty, applicants would just need to give a copy of the survey to their building society/bank to get a formal mortgage offer. Under such circumstances the whole transaction could be speeded up enormously, as all that would be left to do once an offer was made would be the legal work. Solicitors and conveyancers would soon come round to the altered circumstances and the result would be an exchange within seven to fourteen days. Thereafter completion could be delayed to allow people to get themselves organised for a move (if required), but they would be safe. Chains would not be obliterated by a speedier contract stage, but such instant commitment is likely to deter people from proceeding until they see both ends to a chain, and the nuisance value of chains would be enormously reduced.

Unfortunately the untransferable liability of surveys prevents this course at present. Both the purchaser and the building society or bank would have no comeback on a negligent survey that was carried out for the vendor, but surely it is not beyond the capability of the professionals to provide the increased liability even if it means the cost would be raised a little? If the huge chains of agents agreed to implement the new system by not taking unprepared instructions, the uncertainties of today's procedures would seem laughable within a few years.

Multi-listing is another rising star in the firmament that has gone beyond the conceptual stage and is becoming a reality in some areas.

In its fully evolved form this is a system whereby information on all properties on the market in an area is available on a central computer that can be accessed by any participating agent who has a suitable prospective purchaser. The level of personal service to the vendor is retained as all appointments have to go through the instructed agent and he alone has the right to advertise. The agent finding a buyer and the instructed agent share the fee between them.

The advantages are manifold. The vendor gets very wide coverage for his property, and can feel secure in the knowledge that the market has been well and truly covered when accepting offers. The applicant need no longer pound the streets of town and city but will feel confident he is getting a full representation of properties of interest to him. He will be able to deal with an agent he feels comfortable with as opposed to the haphazard system of the present. From the estate agent's point of view, it makes sole agency the norm, thereby enabling him to concentrate his resources and time more efficiently and reducing the chances of gazumping. The agent will also be able to devote more time to the serious buyers in the market, no longer having to watch such people leave his office disappointed because he has nothing to offer within his limited range of properties.

It could be a while before multi-listing becomes standard practice in the U.K. but already forward-looking businessmen and estate agents are promoting it as a genuine aid to all concerned with property transactions. A greater degree of self-regulation and a raising of standards generally are likely to be among the benefits. There is every reason to suppose that the huge chains of agents will want to participate as they are likely to want to improve the service available to the public and multi-listing creates no conflict with their interests. Some agents are still wary but most will agree that the concept is sound. Multi-listing requires a greater degree of trust and co-operation between agents than exists at present, although they already work together more than is generally realised. The inefficiencies of the current system make the effort well worthwhile.

So that is my two penny worth. In the meantime I hope the practical aspects of this book will help you through the minefield of our current system.

Good Luck.

INDEX

OTHER GREAT PAPERFRONT BOOKS

Each uniform with this book

WRITE YOUR OWN WILL

Keith Best's book contains all you need to make a proper legal Will yourself. Sample Wills designed to cover most circumstances are included. If you are wealthy, or your affairs are complicated, then you should consult a solicitor about your Will after reading this book, which will guide you as to the questions you should ask.

PROBATE: THE RIGHT WAY TO PROVE A WILL

Keith Best explains clearly and concisely how to apply for Probate (or Letters of Administration if there is no Will) and how to administer the Estate. He lays down the sequence of things to do, and gives some basic advice on more technical matters. The help of a solicitor is not necessary for the majority of simple Estates, but the reader is clearly told when it may be needed.

DIVORCE – The Things You Thought You'd Never Need To Know

Jill Black, barrister and law lecturer, steers the reader calmly and sympathetically through the 'minefield' of divorce. She explains the usual sequence of events, and how things are set in motion. Some case histories and a broad insight into how the courts make their decisions help the reader to appreciate what to expect in his or her own circumstances.

WHAT TO DO WHEN SOMEONE HAS DEBT PROBLEMS

John McQueen shows you how to move fast and objectively, to delay the claims against you and guide you back to solvency. The legal realities are explained through case histories and experiences of the hundreds of people he has helped since he founded the Association of Bankrupts.

ELLIOT RIGHT WAY BOOKS
KINGSWOOD, SURREY, U.K.

OUR PUBLISHING POLICY

HOW WE CHOOSE

Our policy is to consider every deserving manuscript and we can give special editorial help where an author is an authority on his subject but an inexperienced writer. We are rigorously selective in the choice of books we publish. We set the highest standards of editorial quality and accuracy. This means that a *Paperfront* is easy to understand and delightful to read. Where illustrations are necessary to convey points of detail, these are drawn up by a subject specialist artist from our panel.

HOW WE KEEP PRICES LOW

We aim for the big seller. This enables us to order enormous print runs and achieve the lowest price for you. Unfortunately, this means that you will not find in the *Paperfront* list any titles on obscure subjects of minority interest only. These could not be printed in large enough quantities to be sold for the low price at which we offer this series. We sell almost all our *Paperfronts* at the same unit price. This saves a lot of fiddling about in our clerical departments and helps us to give you world-beating value. Under this system, the longer titles are offered at a price which we believe to be unmatched by any publisher in the world.

OUR DISTRIBUTION SYSTEM

Because of the competitive price, and the rapid turnover, *Paperfronts* are possibly the most profitable line a bookseller can handle. They are stocked by the best bookshops all over the world. It may be that your bookseller has run out of stock of a particular title. If so, he can order more from us at any time – we have a fine reputation for 'same day' despatch, and we supply any order, however small (even a single copy), to any bookseller who has an account with us. We prefer you to buy from your bookseller, as this reminds him of the strong underlying public demand for *Paperfronts*. Members of the public who live in remote places, or who are housebound, or whose local bookseller is unco-operative, can order direct from us by post.

FREE

If you would like an up-to-date list of all paperfront titles currently available, send a stamped self-addressed envelope to
ELLIOT RIGHT WAY BOOKS, BRIGHTON RD.,
LOWER KINGSWOOD, SURREY, U.K.